CATCH CARP

THE ANGLING TIMES LIBRARY

CATCH CARP

WITH

JOHN WILSON

B🌿XTREE

in association with
ANGLING TIMES

First published in Great Britain in 1991 by Boxtree Limited
This paperback edition first published in 1994

3 5 7 9 10 8 6 4 2

Angling Times is a weekly newspaper produced by EMAP
Publishing Limited, Bretton, Peterborough. Established
in 1953, it is Britain's biggest selling weekly fishing
publication.

Illustrations by David Batten
Cover designed by Geoff Hayes
Colour origination by Fotographics, Hong Kong
Printed and bound in the UK by Cambus Litho Ltd for

Boxtree Limited
Broadwall House
21 Broadwall
London SE1 9PL

A CIP catalogue entry for this book is available from the
British Library.

ISBN 0 7522 1098 X

CONTENTS

ACKNOWLEDGEMENTS

No angling writer can produce a book without considerable help from others. Allow me therefore to thank the editing and design team, the mates who leave their own fishing to photograph me, and a very special thank you to good friend Dave Batten who has made such a fine job of the line drawings.

John Wilson
Great Witchingham
1991

INTRODUCTION

ONLY 35 years ago, back in the mid 1950s, most anglers simply talked about the mystique surrounding carp, few actually ever saw the fish in their landing-net. Today the situation has been completely reversed as more and more fisheries become stocked with this exciting species. Carp are now the most sought after freshwater fish in Britain, surpassing in popularity even the roach. The reasons for this are not difficult to understand. Carp quickly grow to a large size, providing everyone with their best chance of coming to grips with a fish of 10 lb and more. They fight harder than all other species found in both still and running water, with the exception of perhaps salmon and catfish. And they are not difficult to catch when stocked in reasonable numbers. What is more, being a durable, long-living creature they are the 'perfect' stock fish guaranteed to provide fishery owners with value for money and anglers with a powerful adversary whether it weighs 3 lb or 30 lb. And this surely is the carp's real strength. Whatever its size, it provides a thrilling battle.

This book is about my ways of catching carp and subsequently enjoying catching carp of all sizes. It is not a manual for those interested only in monster specimens, which require much dedication and a single-minded approach. I make no secret of the fact that I have yet to find enough time to pursue this goal. To many, carp fishing is about putting up a bivi for the weekend, casting out a couple of ledgered baits and sitting back waiting for runs to develop. It is not my idea of carp fishing. I simply haven't the time. My carp are invariably caught during short pre-work sessions or perhaps in the evening as the light starts to go, and occasionally at midday. I simply enjoy the never-ending challenge of catching carp of different colours and strains and of different sizes and scale patterns from a wide variety of interesting fisheries. I value tremendously the battle of a 20-pounder when it finally lies there glistening in the net after a long stalking session. But I am also just as happy banging into 3 lb wildies or pound-plus crucians one after another on light float tackle. It is all relative.

I hope therefore the reader can share my approach

within the pages of this book, which is far from and in no way pretends to be a complete work on the subject, and quite simply 'catch carp with me'. Perhaps we'll both learn a little along the way.

CHAPTER ONE

THE
SPECIES

WILD CARP
(Cyprinus carpio)

Pound for pound there are few fish living in stillwaters to match the speed and the power of the true wild carp. They originated from Eastern Europe and Asia, where the Chinese were the first to cultivate them for food several hundred years before Christ. It was the European monks, however, who brought the species to Britain to rear them in stew ponds for their table. And it is that same race of carp which we today lovingly call 'wildies' or wild carp.

Who knows, one day 'wildie waters' may become a very rare commodity and expensive to fish, because over the years the true wildie has slowly been losing its identity, as more and more fisheries are stocked with the deeper-bodied, heavier and faster-growing strains of king carp.

Although there are slight genetic differences between 'wild' and common, scaled 'king' carp there are no apparent visual differences other than shape. A particularly thin king common, for instance, might just be mistaken for a true wildie (in waters where both exist) while an over-fed wildie can look remarkably like an under-nourished king common. If you are confused you have every right to be, because unless a particular fishery is known to contain only an ancient stock of wild carp to which no other strains have been added, the exact definition of the inhabitants becomes arguable.

However, as there are no separate UK record lists for wild carp – simply 'carp' – regardless of scaleage and ancestry, it really matters not. In any event ultimate weight is nothing like that of the king varieties inhabiting the warmest parts of Europe. Wildies in Britain which weigh in excess of 10 lb are as rare as the proverbial clockwork orange, because the species tends to over-

This long, lean, fully-scaled carp epitomizes the barbel-like shape of the true 'wildie' or wild carp. The true 'wildie' has slowly been losing its identity as more fisheries are stocked with deeper-bodied, faster-growing strains of king carp variants.

populate the shallow, coloured waters where it fares best; farm ponds and irrigation reservoirs being prime examples.

Generally this sleek, barbel-shaped carp averages between 2 and 5 lb as an adult in prolific waters, though naturally fisheries with a lower stock density will produce fish of a higher average size provided the food source is sufficient.

The very reason why wild carp were chosen as an important food source in the first place was that even in overcrowded shallow waters they made the very best of the available food supply and produced per acre far more pounds of edible flesh than any other species.

Presumably for this very reason the same carp was introduced to North America in the 1800s and spread the width and breadth of the continent by the Great Western Railway. Unfortunately, unlike in Europe, carp has never caught on in the USA or Canada as a human food source. Nor has it in the UK, although those of Jewish, Polish, German and Hungarian descent do provide a small market for imported and home-grown table carp.

So 'anti carp' are anglers in the USA and Canada that the fish only rates as enjoyment for lunatics pursuing it with bow and arrow. An abundance of exciting sport-fish species North America may well have, but it is a great pity her fishermen have yet to value the gift of the carp.

When fishing the Red River in Winnipeg, Canada,

during the summers of 1989 and 1990 for the hard-battling channel catfish, I was flabbergasted to hear from my guide, Stu Makay, who runs a tackle business out of Lockport Bridge Dam, that as yet no one has bothered to exploit the fighting potential of the carp as a sport fish in the Red River system. Yet, with its maze of shallow marshlands off the main channel covering hundreds of thousands of acres of water, averaging over 70°F during the summer months, carp are present in unbelievable quantities over 10 lb, and up to 40 lb or more. And they never see a baited hook. Walleye to over 10 lb, white bass to 3 lb, catfish to 30 lb, and various smaller species which make up the fishing potential of the Red River are all held in the highest esteem. But carp – sadly they are considered nothing but vermin.

In Australia, where the introduction of carp to clear, weedy rivers has completely altered the balance and affected the spawning of indigenous species, there is a hefty fine for anyone returning a carp. A similar situation exists in New Zealand, where carp are now breeding prolifically in the ideal conditions of warm, shallow and weedy, slow-moving river systems.

Small, attractively matured, man-made fisheries originating from gravel excavations are an exciting part of the future of carp fishing within the British Isles.

THE KING CARPS
(Cyprinus carpio)

From the original wild carp, different strains have been produced by selective breeding throughout Europe during the past three centuries. In order for the European housewife to be presented with a fast-growing, deep-shouldered table carp, which in some cases (the leather carp) alleviates even the need for descaling, fish culturists have evolved the king carp. This durable carp, due to its fast-growing qualities, massive ultimate weight and attractive scale patterns, forms the basis of British carp fishing as we know it today. For this we owe Germany, Poland, Yugoslavia and Hungary much gratitude. In recent years the Belgians, Israelies, Italians and French have also got in on the act, adding still more variants within the king carp range.

Ultimate weight for a king carp is still uncertain. Monsters of 80 lb plus have been recorded so there is every reason to expect that in the right growing conditions a king carp in excess of 100 lb will one day be taken on rod and line from European waters. In Britain our summers do not get hot enough and are too short for such monsters to be produced, and it is doubtful whether the present ceiling weight of 50 lb will ever be substantially increased. But then with global warming imminent, who really knows for sure.

One of the nicest by-products to come from the selective breeding of king carp strains is the amount of varying scale patterns that occur between the fully-scaled king common carp and the completely scaleless leather carp. We anglers love to catch beautiful fish and the king carp varieties provide both interest and beauty. Carp specialists would perhaps argue about exactly how many varying scaleages can be separately categorized, but there are several distinct patterns. There is of course no way of describing them all, but the following are easily recognizable.

THE KING COMMON CARP is the fully-scaled modern equivalent of the original wild carp, selectively bred to be thicker across the body, deeper and much faster growing with a far greater weight potential.

THE FULLY-SCALED MIRROR, being completely covered in scales of different sizes, is by far the prettiest and possibly the most desirable to catch of all the variants.

THE SCATTER-SCALE MIRROR generally has a continuous line of scales on both sides of the dorsal fin from head to tail, with single or odd groups appearing almost anywhere, particularly close to the tail root or head, or both. By far the most common form of mirror carp.

THE LINEAR MIRROR is known for its straight row of uniform scales along the lateral line, plus odd groups near the tail and on both sides of the dorsal fin.

THE STARBURST MIRROR is really a scatter-scale mirror with a preponderance of tiny, bright scales shot all over the lower half of its body. Italian goldfish and shubunkins have very similar scaleage, reminiscent of a burst of stars – hence this particular carp's nickname.

THE PLATED MIRROR again is really a scatter-scale fish with anything from one to several enormous plate-like scales set in an irregular-shaped group on one or both sides of its body. Not a fish that wears well in a busy fishery, because during the fight the line can catch behind these big scales and force them out.

THE LEATHER CARP is completely free of scales over the body with perhaps the odd line of small scales either side of the dorsal fin.

In addition to scaleage the king carp varies considerably in body shape, but usually has a distinct and characteristic hump between its head and dorsal fin. Those without a hump probably have some wild carp in their ancestry. Certain strains may be long and incredibly thick across the body without having much of an obvious belly, whilst others come short and deep with enormous pot bellies. In truth, there is so much cross-breeding now taking place in the wild as carp propagate all over the country that it would take an experienced carp culturist to be dogmatic about which is truly which. But then the fun of carp fishing lies in fishing waters where you never know what will be coming along next, in size, in shape, in scaleage and even in colour.

Steve Williams from Norwich has every right to look pleased with his capture. This beautifully marked, fully-scaled mirror was caught from a large, heavily reeded Norfolk gravel pit.

COLORATION

Genetic differences apart, colour variation is to some extent governed by the colour of water in which carp live. In sandy or green-pea coloured fisheries, for instance, body coloration often fades to an overall pale, pasty cast in either beige, grey or dull brass with a distinct warm tinge to the tail, pelvic and anal fins. This applies to both wild and king carp, whereas carp inhabiting lush, weedy, clear-watered fisheries can vary along the back from bronze to slate blue, with scales of burnished pewter, gold or silver. The fins will still contain a certain warmth together with hues of grey, purple and beige.

COLOURED VARIANTS
(Metallic Carp)

Actually catching on hook and line a valuable, highly-coloured koi carp would have been unthinkable prior to the mid-1980s. But now, stillwater horizons have broadened due to the general deterioration of river systems caused by abstraction, farming chemicals and increased amounts of sewage effluent. Anglers are ready to accept that king carp/koi crosses or even true koi carp (koi simply

means coloured) can provide exciting sport with beautiful, hard-fighting fish in selected waters. After all, the coloured carps are genetically no different from the original wild carp and share the same latin species name of *cyprinus carpio*.

The Japanese first developed strains of coloured carp, today known as koi. And although there are references in Japanese literature to coloured ornamentals dating back as early as AD 714, the origin of coloured carp is generally accepted to go back to the Hei-an period 794–1184.

Because stillwater fisheries have extended the range of species that they stock over recent years, more and more anglers are now ready to accept that beautiful, hard-fighting fish like this beige-coloured king carp/koi cross can provide exciting sport.

Whatever the scale-age and pigmentation, genetically there is no difference between this beautiful orange hi-goi and all other carp. They all share the Latin name of Cyprinus carpio *and interbreed freely, throwing up all sorts of exciting variations.*

By the Middle Ages, during the Momyama Era from 1582 to 1598, koi culture became popular throughout Japan. Anglers who now have the opportunity of hooking into a koi/king carp cross, the most common of which are called Ghost Koi at fish and garden centres, really have the Japanese to thank.

This stunning breed of 'metallic' carp, so called because most colours suitable for stocking fisheries come in muted shades of metallic pewter, silver, pale gold and burnished beige, are indeed an exciting and extremely durable addition to specialist carp waters.

I stocked metallic carp into my own lakes during the early 1980s and have been more than pleased with the results. Not only do they add another challenge in the range of colour, but seem to know they are 'coloured' and thus more visible. Rarely do the metallics slurp around with their head and shoulders above the surface as uncoloured king carp often do, consuming vast quantities of floaters. Their whole approach – and I can only believe after 10 years of monitoring their antics day in and day out from March to November, that this is typical of metallics – is much more wary. Thus they offer a tremendous challenge, and an alternative to those anglers who fall into the trap of focussing only on the very largest carp, thus denying themselves a glimpse of a breathtakingly coloured 'metallic' in the mesh of their landing-net.

GRASS CARP
(Ctenopharyngoden idella)

This Asian import, which originates from China, adds another exciting chapter to modern stillwater carp fishing, though in appearance the grass carp resembles the chub very closely indeed. Unless its eyes and mouth can be clearly seen, only the fact that it loves to hover just beneath the surface with its head tilted upwards visually distinguishes this sleek battler from chub. Beneath the surface, its tail may also appear to be both darker and slightly larger than that of the chub, but in scaleage they look exactly the same.

The big give-away occurs when it turns head on and

opens its noticeably smaller mouth. The eyes look distinctly odd too. They are in fact set much lower down the head, on a line only just above the jaw hinge.

Grass carp are far from the marauding weed-eaters and nautical lawnmowers they were made out to be when first introduced to the UK. Here, so it seemed, was the answer to everyone's prayers at last, the panacea for anyone who owned a pond or lake dogged with soft weeds. Stock it with a few grass carp and the weeds would be nicely kept in trim – ravaged even.

At least, this was the message from local river authorities and what a load of rubbish it turned out to be. British summers are never long enough, and the water temperature rarely stays high enough for long enough, for the grass carp to become an effective weed-disposal unit. Certainly they consume weed but then so do most cyprinids. The truth is that grass carp are timid when stocked in small numbers into a mature fishery that already contains a prolific stock of king carp, and they always get to the bait last. As they love to feed from the surface, floater-fishing with baits like bread crust or flake on freeline tackle offers the best chance of being selective. They feed from the bottom too, and will accept most common carp baits such as peanuts, boilies, sweetcorn, luncheon meat and so on.

Even when stocked into fisheries that are already densely populated, they will pack on weight and grow to at least double figures within six or seven years. In rich, under-populated stillwaters and rivers, their growth could almost equal that of other carp, and an estimate of 20 lb-plus is not unrealistic.

In Germany, where the grass carp was introduced years ahead of the UK, 40 lb grass carp are not uncommon. As they tend to scrap very well indeed, making long runs close to the surface, who would not fancy the chances of contacting one. Grass carp are the perfect controllable carp for stocking the fisheries of today, because they cannot reproduce in our climate and over-populate a water. As yet, they have not been stocked on a widespread basis, but once fishery owners learn to appreciate their real worth anglers will enjoy them.

It may well be the case in many parts of the country that fishery owners are not even aware that this fine fish exists and that it can be purchased for stocking.

Chub-like in appearance, the enigmatic grass carp freely accept both bottom and surface baits. The downfall of this incredibly long 11-pounder was a small dog-biscuit floater presented on a weighted controller and greased line.

CRUCIAN CARP
(Carassius carassius)

The crucian carp was introduced to the UK sometime during the eighteenth century and has established itself, particularly amongst young anglers, as a popular summer pond fish. It is by far the smallest member of the 'angling carps', rarely exceeding 5 lb. Even this, however, is exceptional. Crucian carp of over 2 lb are considered large specimens because, due to over-breeding, the species becomes stunted and in many waters rarely grows above 12 oz and 10 in in length. This cheeky little carp is noticeably short and deep with distinctly 'rounded' fins. The dorsal is also rounded and convex, in complete contrast to the dorsal fin of other carps which is concave.

The crucian has a small, neat mouth and barbules are absent – one sure way of differentiating between it and either wild or king carp. Coloration tends to vary from one water to another, just like other carp. But they are

Gentle, golden, friendly and decidedly rounded in both body and fins, the crucian might well be the smallest carp around, but it fights doggedly and provides great fun on light tackle.

coloured very evenly in an overall hue of bronze, dull gold or buttery bronze. The fins are also very evenly coloured.

The curious thing about crucians is that they like to shoal in definite age or year groups. So if you catch one weighing, say, 1 1/4 lb followed by a dozen more, there is an excellent chance that each will be more or less of the same stamp.

This 'peas in the pod' phenomenon can prove a valuable guideline for those seeking out a net full of specimens, though naturally as the fish grow larger the size of the shoal slowly reduces.

CHAPTER TWO

ABOUT CARP

FEEDING

Carp have been likened to aquatic pigs, which is not so very far from the truth. They are by far the most aggressive feeders in freshwater. During a five-month period throughout the winter I reared on in a large, heated aquarium 11 Wels catfish and one mirror carp. Each was around 3 to 4 in long when put in, along with rocks, plants, and sections of drainpipe as refuge for the catfish. I was concerned that the cats would dominate the food introduced, which initially consisted of high protein salmon-fry crumbs, followed by a completely live-fish diet, small gudgeon in fact, netted from the lake into which the cats and carp eventually went.

Invariably it was the lone carp and not the cats which got to the food first – both granulated and live. I was flabbergasted when the first batch of inch-long gudgeon fry were introduced. The mirror carp zoomed up and swallowed 3 live gudgeon before the cats even saw them, and this was more or less what happened every few days at feeding time until I released them into their new home in the spring. By then the cats varied between 11 and 14 in in length and the carp was around 10 in though it was fatter and weighed slightly more than the longest cat. In the wild, wherever both carp and catfish exist together, it is always carp which dominate the available food source and reach your bait first. The balance swings slightly more towards catfish only during darkness, when they naturally become more active, and during high water temperatures – say 70°F and above. But overall and compared to all other freshwater species in Europe, possibly the whole world over, the carp really is the pig of the aquatic scene.

Having said all this, the non-angler may well ask the question, 'Why at times do they become so difficult to catch?' The answer is, that they learn. While carp are not the most intelligent of fish as has been suggested by many specialist fishermen, they quickly learn through association (as all fish do) exactly what to be suspicious about. Baits they have recently been caught on and thus fooled by, over-thick line, insensitive terminal rigs, shadows on the water, unnatural sounds picked up through bank vibrations and so on; these and many other factors, once the carp learns to associate each with danger, are enough to deter it from feeding naturally in its piggy, aggressive way.

I recall an occasion which illustrates this perfectly. During the close season, Neil Pope and Kevin Wilmot from *Angling Times* had arrived at the house to tape part of a series of articles. It was early evening and before we got stuck in around the kitchen table they asked if we could go and feed the carp, something I like to do during the close season to make sure the stock is in good shape for 16th June; and also, I admit, because I simply love to watch fish feeding from the surface. These are carp which for nine months of the year are regularly caught by my 20 syndicate members, but once the close season starts, it doesn't take them long to react to an entirely different set of rules. However, as I walked on ahead to the lake a group of mallards flew from the front lawn to a certain spot on the surface in front of a high, gorse-covered bank, where I stopped. The same spot where, every morning and evening, I throw in a few pints of trout pellets or a bag of old bread scraps.

The carp in the immediate vicinity fully associated the ducks' sudden flight to this particular spot with instant food and quickly gathered around directly beneath them, standing on their tails, mouths open and ready to go. Even before I handed out any pellets or bread scraps, bow waves of additional carp heading through the surface in our direction could be seen on both sides down the lake for as far away as 80 yd. Noise and vibrations travel quickly under water and carp have ears. These distant fish could not possibly have seen or heard *our* arrival 15 ft above, standing well back on the high banking. They were simply reacting to a chain of events, prompted by the arrival of the ducks on the surface at a certain spot and the subsequent movements of other carp to food.

Neil and Kevin stood there absolutely dumbfounded,

There is no doubt about the purpose of the carp's mouth. Complete with thick-rimmed lips and long probing barbules for burrowing deep into the silt to 'feel' for bloodworms and other goodies, it is built to rip the bottom up and turn over vast quantities of organic waste.

obviously assuming I had mystical powers – until I let them in on the situation. After all, no-one expects carp that are caught regularly to appear so quickly. Nevertheless, it's back to square one again on 16th June because suddenly food is being thrown in all over the lake (after being unoccupied for at least three months), and most swims also suddenly have rods hanging threateningly out over the marginal cover. It then takes but a day or two for the fish to revert back to the status quo and to become suspicious again of free food.

This is why you need to be especially stealthy and well camouflaged when tackling previously unfished waters (so-called 'private' lakes where everyone thinks carp crawl up the rods), because if those fish rarely see humans or hear their disturbance along the banks they will be doubly alarmed.

Whilst the carp is capable of obtaining nourishment from almost any food form we offer it, even large baits, its natural diet mostly consists of minute life forms. With its

two pairs of barbules – one long pair at the corner of the mouth, which is protusible, and the other, short ones on the upper lip – the carp is a past master at seeking out midge larvae (blood worms) and annelid worms from the deepest silt concentrations. Deep craters 3 to 6 ft across can sometimes be observed through the clear water of shallow, silty lakes, where concentrations of midge larvae are richest. The carp have simply excavated them whilst feeding, their head and shoulders almost buried while the barbules, which have sensitive taste pads at the tips, 'feel' for the worms. Occasionally a carp may come up to the surface to take floaters, covered in fine mud all over its head; proof that shortly before, it was merrily rooting about in the silt with its head buried, feeding on midge larvae and sending those tell-tale feeding bubbles up to the surface.

These bubbles are caused by two things: gases which escape from the detritus (the rotting layer of vegetation on the bottom); and those created by the carp itself as it crushes up its food with its pharyngeal teeth (throat teeth), emitting the bubbles through its gills. Observing the bubbles of feeding carp is one of the most accurate ways of locating them and arranging subsequent bait presentation (more about this in 'Locating Carp').

When sifting through bottom silt in the early morning, carp send streams of bubbles up to the surface. Follow the route of individual fish feeding at close range, and you can catch them on a simple float rig by casting a little to one side of the rising bubbles.

The carp also uses its flat, immensely powerful pharyngeal teeth for crushing the shells of molluscs upon which it feeds – the tiny pea mussel, snails and even the considerably larger swan mussel. Shells of 2 to 3 in long are light work for the carp's throat teeth, releasing the succulent meat inside. Small dead and live fish up to 6 in long are also easily minced, as anglers offering them after dark with the intention of luring catfish or eels have discovered.

In prolifically stocked waters, especially where competition for the natural aquatic food is high, carp consume far more fish than most anglers could imagine. During the spawning season it is natural for them to munch away on both the spawn and newly-hatched fry. And this does not stop them from enjoying larger 'small fish' either dead or alive at any time of the year. In North America during the summer months, when water temperatures are considerably higher than in the UK, carp are caught regularly on spinners, spoons and jigs, suggesting perhaps that they become more aggressive predators the warmer the water becomes.

Other favourite natural foods are all aquatic insects and beetles, shrimps, assellus and a certain amount of algae from silt and mud on the bottom. They will also gorge on the largest of the zoo planktons, the daphnia, when they are present in thick clouds. As a food converter the carp surpasses even the gluttony of the trout.

Crucians

By comparison with both wild and king carp, the crucian is very timid and deliberate in its feeding. Its diet is not dissimilar to the larger carp at the smaller end of the food chain, and it manages to eke out a living and even to compete with them in densely populated fisheries. I know of many so called 'fast' carp waters which are densely populated with either wildies, king carp or both, but where only crucian carp appear to maintain their existence in quite bagable numbers, whereas either tench or bream as a second species would simply be eaten out of house and home by the larger carp. Perhaps the crucians are simply better at exploiting the smaller food chains than all the other species. They can bite oh-so-gently however, even on light float tackle.

Owing to the crucian carp's slightly upturned mouth structure, they need to stand on their heads (just like the tench) when sucking up food from the bottom. And on chewing it with their pharyngeal teeth they emit distinctive 'crucian bubbles', which rise to the surface in small groups. Ardent crucian fishermen could not mistake these bubbles for any other fish. The bubbles probably fall halfway between those of tench and the larger carps in size, and are never 'frothy'.

REPRODUCTION

In the British Isles carp have the capacity to spawn at any time between early May and the end of July, depending on water temperature. In sheltered, shallow lakes not affected by cold winds, for instance, where the water warms quickly, carp are most likely to spawn early. Whereas in large open and very deep-watered gravel pits which take a long time to warm up, spawning may not occur until even the end of July. This of course makes a nonsense of the dates for the statutory close season, because it is mostly water temperature which prompts fish to shed their eggs.

It is perhaps a blessing in disguise that in the UK a large percentage of the spawn does not reach adulthood, which is far from the case in countries like Australia, North America and Spain for instance, or our fisheries would simply be overrun with carp to the detriment of other species.

When spawning occurs, the spectator can have little doubt it is happening. It is a very noisy event, particularly when every fish in the lake seems bent on propagation at the same time. Propagation usually starts in the early hours and continues until the sun gets high; it may resume again during the evening. The activity continues every morning for several days, unless the weather changes drastically with a sharp fall in temperature. Then spawning ceases, sometimes for many weeks, until carp feel the urge again, stimulated by a steady rise in water temperature.

During poor summers and continually long cold spells

The carp's pharyngeal teeth are situated between its gill plates at the back of the throat, and are used for grinding food to a pulp. This pair was taken from a dead fish slightly larger than the mirror carp shown here.

some females never get to shed their eggs, resulting in hideous pot-bellied fish which can eventually die from their spawn-bound condition unless they manage to re-absorb the eggs into their system. Each ripe female is usually accompanied by anywhere from two to several males, all eager to spray milt over the eggs as she sheds them amongst the fibrous sub-surface roots of marginal trees, through rushes, sedges, reeds, lilies, soft weeds and so on. This is accompanied by much audible shuddering and splashing as the entwining carp crash their way through marginal vegetation where the water is warmest. Such is the force of the males' attention that the female is often lifted bodily out of the water, while the odd over-zealous male can even find itself high and dry on the bank.

The sticky eggs are each about the size of a no. 8 split shot, and are a translucent pale colour unless they failed to receive milt from the male, in which case they remain unfertilized and quickly turn white. Eggs that are not quickly consumed by shoals of small roach, perch or rudd, which follow the spawning carp in anticipation, or by the carp themselves, hatch some six to ten days later. Again this depends on the amount of sunlight and subsequent water

temperature. The newly-hatched fry have yolk sacks to feed on for two to four days before coming to the surface and filling their swim bladders with air. They then become free swimming and commence feeding on microscopic life.

If a lake contains a varied stock of mixed carp, inter-breeding occurs when they all get together at spawning time. Wildies spawn with kings, crucians with wildies, wildies with metallic king mirrors or leather or commons, and so on.

The wildie/crucian carp cross matures into an interesting fish which appears slightly too deep to be the true wildie everyone assumes it is, the give-away being its noticeably smaller barbules and an overall paler coloration.

The most attractive crosses of all come from the metallic carps with koi ancestry locked up in their genes. Most of the brightest ones never get beyond the fry stage. Being far more visible than the rest, they soon fall prey to the stealthy heron and predatory fish. But those that are only slightly tinted over the body and on the underside of the pectoral and pelvic fins in shades of muted silver and beige turn into breathtaking carp, particularly those with mirror scaleage.

Carp in the British Isles are so interbred that with most it is virtually impossible to state the exact parentage. This golden metallic mirror cross, however, obviously has koi ancestry.

DISTRIBUTION

Although there are still 'wildie only' waters in Wales, southern England and the Midlands, few exist in Scotland and Ireland. On the other hand, king carp and their variants are now being stocked into just about every new lake or gravel pit fishery through the North, the Midlands and southern England. Not that carp really need any help at this stage. They have steadily spread (and not always by the design of water authorities) into numerous river systems all over the country. The Trent, Thames and the Great Ouse are prime examples where carp are now so prolific in certain stretches that anglers can actually pick a swim known for producing numbers of them, something that was virtually unheard of in this country's rivers only 20 years ago.

The crucian does not spread so readily, and fares poorly in running water. It is, however, becoming increasingly popular amongst match and club fishermen because it is extremely durable, and it exists in prolific numbers even in diminutive stillwater fisheries.

CHAPTER THREE

LOCATING CARP

M AKE no mistake about it, carp location is what catching them is really all about. After all, if there are none where you place the bait, you can't catch them. So be willing, and this applies in particular to fisheries low in carp stocks and large areas of water, to spend more hours in locating the fish than you do actually fishing.

Tools of the trade, as important as the rod and reel, are polaroid glasses, binoculars, drab clothing and lightweight boots, whether waterproof or not, so that from the very start your approach is not at fault. The importance of being quiet, stealthy and unseen against the skyline cannot be stressed enough if you wish to find and subsequently study your quarry before offering it a bait. When you can creep up (crawl if necessary) to within a few feet of carp, or watch them swim close by without their having the slightest inkling of your presence, you should then be qualified to catch them from any type of water. No other fish except the chub demands such cautionary measures but it is an apprenticeship in watercraft that when learnt will last a lifetime.

SMALL STILLWATERS

Where carp cannot be bodily observed because the water is too coloured or temperatures too cold for them to be basking on the surface, there are many pointers to look for. Fortunately carp love features, gravel bars, sunken trees, lily pads, reedlines, etc., and are never far away. In diminutive waters, ponds, pits, meres, lakes – those for argument's sake of less than 3 acres (a football pitch is about 1 acre) – carp are not difficult to locate, and are fun

Careful observation is paramount if you wish to catch carp with regularity from a wide range of stillwaters. Owning a pair of binoculars and climbing the occasional tree is not cheating, but be careful.

to study. Nearly always they can be visually tracked down during the summer months. The most obvious indication of fish is the characteristic way in which carp 'bubble' (see 'Feeding'). Their 'feeding bubbles', which could occur at any time of the day (especially during overcast, humid, thundery oppressive summer weather), are most likely to appear coinciding with dawn. They could well then continue until the sun's rays fall directly on the water. This post-dawn feeding period is by far the heaviest. More importantly, it pin-points areas which carp visit often, usually on a day-to-day basis, and most important of all where they feed 'naturally'.

Simply taking time for a stealthy stroll with a pair of binoculars at dawn can provide so much information, far more in fact than an entire week of midday sessions. What stands out when observing 'bubbles' is that many natural feeding areas are situated ridiculously close in. That's because shallow water warms up quickly and invariably contains per square foot a much richer larder of natural food, a fact of which carp quickly become aware. This is the reason margin fishing under quiet conditions can prove

so effective. Why so many carp fishermen cast right over to the other bank when they could just as easily (probably more effectively too) walk round and catch the same fish beneath the rod tip on considerably lighter, more enjoyable tackle, is completely beyond my comprehension. Certainly, once they have been scared away from their preferred haunts a long cast is necessary to offer them a bait. The object, however, is not to scare them away in the first place.

Find lilies and you will find carp. In this green jungle, amongst a mixture of dwarf pond lily and large pads of the common yellow water lily, a fat mirror and a mallard cross see who can reach the floaters first.

Lilies

Lily-beds, the thicker the better, are the most popular of the carp's daytime haunts, especially in waters with little protection to offer in the way of overhanging trees and marginal growth. The shade provided by pads overhead and a maze of roots below, to which a rich supply of snails and their eggs adhere, makes these sub-surface vegetable gardens very attractive.

Fortunately, the vast majority of anglers feel inhibited about trying to extract such a large fish as carp from dense vegetation, so thick beds of lilies remain largely unexplored. The ideal outfit consists of a stretchy line and all-through-action rod for subduing the heavy lunges of a hooked fish.

Whether carp are present or not is sometimes plainly obvious, their wide backs pushing pads, flowers and stalks aside as they forage beneath. There will be occasions, however, when it seems there isn't a carp anywhere near the lilies. However, take a long slow look. Don't trust the naked eye; rely on the magnification provided by binoculars, even for scanning beds of lilies situated close in. Look for the single flower stalk that sways gently when there is no wind; for large bubbles rising to the surface in groups of just two or three; for the fry shoal which suddenly scatters across the surface, not followed by a predatory perch or pike; for patches of discoloured water (these are evident through polaroids in even the most coloured waters) beneath the pads, alongside or even several yards away.

Climb a suitable tree close by for the best possible view of the situation. If you stay up in the branches long enough and are able to observe carp entering a large bed of lilies, it will eventually become obvious that they go in only at certain spots. These are the wide, naturally formed entrances to the tunnels through the maze of stems and rhyzomes which the carp navigate – worth remembering when you are back down on the ground again, wondering where to plop in a bait.

Owing to its extra, sub-surface leaves, the common yellow water lily (*Nuphar lutea*) is much preferred by carp to the white and coloured cultivated varieties wherever they have a choice. But once hooked, fish are more difficult to extract from the tough stems and enormous entanglement of tubers, which often 'suspend' well above the bottom.

Miniature surface plants such as the dwarf pond lily (easily identified by its buttercup-yellow flowers and perfectly round pads rarely exceeding 3 in across) and the oval-shaped, broad-leaved pond weed (with its erect pink seed-heads protruding above the surface) both also attract carp like bees to a honey pot. Find extensive beds of either smothering the surface of any small (or large) stillwater and expect carp to be foraging beneath at some time during the day, if not all day long.

Sunken/overhanging trees

The presence of carp should always be expected beneath overhanging branches and those which actually trail the surface, because they love a roof over their heads during the hottest, brightest part of a summer's day. Whole trees or large foliage-covered limbs actually sunk below the surface provide fabulous hot spots all year through.

Sunken willows and alders in particular sprout, enormous, fibrous root structures which are teeming with aquatic insect larvae. They provide carp with both food and a retreat where the light from above is always diffused. It is no coincidence that the biggest carp in small waters choose to live in the snaggiest habitats.

Reed lines

Tall marginal plants best loved by carp are the common reed, reed mace (wrongly called bullrush due to its cigar-like seed heads), and the lesser reed mace, a slimmer version. Each will attract carp for the natural food which clings to the upright stems, provided there is a depth of 18 in of water or more. Thick beds of reed which from the front line reach back several yards into marsh bog with pockets of open water in between are great locations, where carp can be expected to browse at any time of the day. And the tall willowy stems even conveniently 'knock' together betraying the presence of any carp moving or feeding between them. Wild carp especially, due to their round profile, are tailor-made for working alongside and through beds of reed.

Gravel bars and shallow plateaux

Owing to the uneven way in which gravel and sand deposits were originally laid down during the last Ice Age, when these minerals are being excavated poor seams are left. Once the pit is allowed to flood from the water table, these seams eventually appear as islands, shallow bars or plateaux. And to each of these carp automatically become

In a quiet corner of a small lake heavily overgrown with branches a sizeable carp buckles the rod, having sucked up the insides of a whole swan mussel freelined beneath the over-hanging foliage. Note how the angler has submerged the rod tip to lower the angle of the line so it stands less chance of snagging, and to apply side strain.

In this swim John practises what he preaches by using the marginal reedline of a shallow, clear-water lake as camouflage. He is offering a bait on the noses of carp that are working close in, feeding on aquatic insects clinging to the upright stems.

attracted. Narrow gaps situated between islands, for instance, could become part of their daily feeding route. Not all, but a proportion of shallow bars will provide either a canopy of floating plants with shelter beneath, or a larder of shrimps and snails amongst the gravel, thus attracting carp. Deeper bars, situated about 4 to 6 ft beneath the surface but 'bars' none the less (where the bottom shelves down to twice the depth or more on either side), are particularly favoured and are ideal locations for pre-baiting. Sometimes these can be seen and pinpointed from the bank through clear water, sometimes not.

Either way, it pays to put in a good amount of reconnaisance work with a plummet (use a boat during the close season if one is allowed at the fishery) when locating carp from a previously unfished or unexplored pit. Discovering the exact whereabouts of all the bars and large areas of plateaux is the absolute key to where carp are most likely to feed naturally.

LARGE STILLWATERS

Though seemingly more daunting because the action of strong winds rippling the surface destroys many of the easily recognizable points which aid location in small fisheries, there is in fact a similarity of approach to tackling the carp of large lakes and gravel pits. And the first step is to think of a large pit as nothing more than a collection of features, just like several small pits joined together. You isolate in your mind (with the help of a drawing if you prefer) all those previously mentioned features to which carp are attracted; the bars, routes between groups of islands, shorelines with dense reed beds, bays harbouring surface plants, overhanging and sunken trees, deep gullies with shallow water on either side and so on. Then spend time with the binoculars during reasonable weather conditions when there is a chance of locating fish visually, not during a raging gale.

A great way of locating carp at any time throughout the summer, especially when it is very warm and they are more liable to be close to the surface of generally deep waters, is to attract them up with floaters. From the

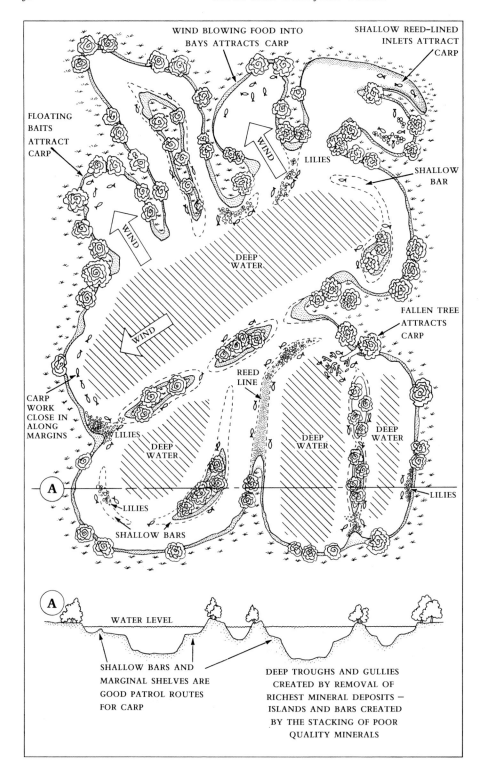

WIND BLOWING FOOD INTO
BAYS ATTRACTS CARP

SHALLOW REED–LINED
INLETS ATTRACT
CARP

FLOATING
BAITS
ATTRACT
CARP

WIND

LILIES

WIND

SHALLOW
BAR

DEEP
WATER

WIND

FALLEN TREE
ATTRACTS
CARP

CARP
WORK
CLOSE IN
ALONG
MARGINS

LILIES

REED
LINE

DEEP
WATER

DEEP
WATER

DEEP
WATER

A

LILIES

DEEP
WATER

LILIES

SHALLOW BARS

A

WATER LEVEL

SHALLOW BARS AND
MARGINAL SHELVES ARE
GOOD PATROL ROUTES
FOR CARP

DEEP TROUGHS AND GULLIES
CREATED BY REMOVAL OF
RICHEST MINERAL DEPOSITS –
ISLANDS AND BARS CREATED
BY THE STACKING OF POOR
QUALITY MINERALS

furthest up-wind position on the bank catapult the surface with small floaters, chum mixers or cat biscuits, and allow the wind to drift this new food source down to the other end of the fishery. Don't be mean during these initial location sessions because they can provide great fun towards the end of the close season when you are itching to see carp. Water birds, like swans, cootes, moorhens and mallards all recognize and come to like floaters unfortunately, so you want enough on the surface to bring the carp up and satisfy the water birds. The presence of birds on the surface enjoying floaters, anyway, is not entirely a bad thing (see 'Feeding'). It gives confidence to the carp below if they are initially hesitant, to a point where eventually they cannot resist getting in on the act. It is that competitive element within all living creatures. Carp may locate and start to feed on the floaters at any time during the drift, especially those which catch up amongst soft weedbeds touching the surface, lilies, or against marginal vegetation. On the other hand, they may not show the slightest interest until the floaters have completed the full length of the fishery and finally come to rest in a scum line hugging the windward shoreline – one very good reason why that old adage of 'fishing into the wind' can prove a winner.

Scumlines

Thick scumlines of pollen, twigs, leaves and other bits formed by the wind blowing from the same direction for several days are great attractors. Natural food including clouds of zooplanktons such as daphnia, plus the remnants of floating fishing baits, are all concentrated in a soup in one area. If this happens to be a shoreline already blessed with features like thick beds of marginal reeds or sedges, lilies or partly submerged trees, it could attract carp in surprising numbers and hold them there until the wind changes direction. On large 'featureless' waters, wind direction alone usually dictates where all small items of natural foods held in suspension near the surface will eventually be deposited. This is why varying areas attract carp only at certain times. These deposits often come to rest on the leeward side of islands and promontories (see

Opposite FIGURE 1
A gravel pit seen from the surface and (bottom) in cross-section, showing the gullies and patrol routes of the carp.

Consisting of leaves,
pollen, twigs and dead
insects, blown into
the margins by
the wind, scumlines
are known for attract-
ing carp. Keeping
down amongst the
foliage, well camou-
flaged by a thick
clump of young alders,
this angler presents
floaters to carp
patrolling the scum-
line.

fig. 1) just as silt in flowing water sinks to the bottom downstream and on the inside of bends where the current always slows down. And whilst the feeding bubbles of carp cannot easily be seen rising in these natural larders at great distances, fish often roll or jump completely clear of the surface when feeding actively and give away their position.

Look closely also for any large 'flat' or calm areas several feet square which suddenly appears amongst the waves. These 'calms' are caused by carp moving beneath the surface without actually breaking it. Such is the force created by their body displacement and powerful fins, the surface tension is 'flattened' long enough for it to be picked up through binoculars even at great distances.

Carp which cannot be seen through really heavily coloured water, even when they feed close in along shallow margins, also indicate their presence through water displacement called 'tail patterns'. These spiral up to the surface in minute vortexes when the carp stands on its head to feed, waggling its tail gently from side to side. Sometimes these 'tail patterns' are accompanied by feeding bubbles and even the fish's body breaking surface, but not always. All are visual indications not to be missed.

Depths

Carp are sometimes stocked into and caught from waters of great depth (20 ft or more) that are completely devoid of shallow areas. However, where they are given a choice of varying depths at which to feed (most waters), I would suggest they prefer to spend a much greater part of their time in less than 12–14 ft of water, rather than deeper water. This is because the greatest concentrations of natural food and choice plant habitats are produced in part by sunlight. And in excessively deep water, particularly if it is heavily coloured (old clay pits and the like), sunlight cannot penetrate down far enough to stimulate growth.

WINTER LOCATION

Though the leaves have gone, over-hanging trees beneath which carp basked all summer are the first spots to try once winter sets in and frosts clear the water. At midday during maximum visibility, their dark shapes can often be seen among the sunken branches.

Many prime summer haunts will still hold carp through-out the winter months, particularly dense habitat areas where partly submerged trees and bushes overhang the margins into deepish water. Deep gullies or troughs in what are generally shallow lakes or pits are also certain to be holding fish.

The much deeper, 'dam' end of man-made estate-type lakes is the obvious choice in continually cold conditions. Even lily beds (or what's left of them) maintain their attraction for carp despite the rotting stalks, and pads not being visible. Always keep a mental note (by lining up a particular tree or gate post on the opposite bank during the summer when the pads are up) as to exactly where the main structure of the plants are situated for winter attention. Carp will always be found amongst it.

RIVER CARP

These are really a law unto themselves. Although they are naturally attracted to all features associated with flowing water, like weir pools, lock cuttings, junctions where side streams join the main flow, mill streams, deep holes on acute bends, beneath overhanging trees and so on, they are completely nomadic, travelling long distances in the course of just a few hours.

Most of the carp in my local Norfolk rivers, the Yare, Wensum and Waveney (which were not intentionally stocked, but contain escapees from fish farms and gravel-pit fisheries adjacent to the rivers) are great wanderers. I have caught them on ledgered bread flake whilst winter chubbing, and right out of the blue during the autumn when barbel fishing swims that have been heavily pre-baited with hemp seed. They are also hooked (and occasionally even landed) by matchmen on casters on maggots designed for roach in the tidal stretches.

In short, one might turn up by itself, or as one of a small group, from just about anywhere and at any time. I have occasionally managed to bag one instantly whilst playing the wandering game for chub, using freelined lobworms in the clear weedy conditions of summer. However, river carp are not keen to respond to an 'instant' meal plopped close by, as chub do. Such offerings are treated with far more suspicion.

River carp do, however, respond wonderfully to regular pre-baiting and this is the most successful way of locating them. The ruse is to pick a few likely habitat-type swims where carp are occasionally seen, and then every other day introduce some loose feed. Stewed wheat, peanuts, maize (don't forget to pressure cook it), black eyed beans and so on (see 'Baits') are all cheap enough to purchase in bulk for heavy and regular baitings. Taking into account the fact that water birds and unwanted species like chub will quickly try and mop up much of the bait, it is pointless putting in just the odd handful. We are talking about something like 3 to 6 pt a go, otherwise you are simply wasting your time and money, as you would be if you used baits such as maggots which every other fish gobbles up long before the carp arrive on the scene.

LOCATING CRUCIANS

This is a most pleasant exercise in the confines of small fisheries (and most crucian waters are small), due to the fact that they conveniently bubble away (see 'Feeding') from dawn onwards between June and September. They feed well into sunlight, even all day through on occasions, so long as the loose feed keeps going in.

They are so obliging and love to porpoise on the surface when in a feeding mood, particularly at dawn and dusk. They are also known for those spectacular jumps completely clear of the surface. Why they do this has never been fully understood, but I have always suspected they are simply ridding themselves of parasites from their gills or scales after sifting through bottom mud and silt.

Look for their distinctive bubbles in warm, shallow to medium-depth swims between beds of any floating-leaved plant, lilies especially (though broad-leaved pond weed, amphibious bistort and dwarf pond lily are also much loved by them) and you will have located the choicest of crucian habitats.

Where there are no lilies, explore just a few feet out from the reedline or close alongside partly submerged bushes

(blackthorn, hawthorn, brambles, etc.) which grow out over the water and actually hang their foliage beneath the surface. Look for definite habitats, but above all from that 'pregnant dawn period' look for those groups of feeding bubbles.

Because crucians, unlike the larger carps, rarely roam to follow food lines, most fisheries have 'known' crucian carp swims or hot spots where these obliging fish reside day in, day out regardless of angling pressure. Mind you, such fish learn to be incredibly crafty, and become the most delicately biting fish in freshwater. So the location of new and not so popular areas is a worthwhile exercise.

Crucian carp love the warm, shallow, lily-shaded water of small lakes, pits and meres. Sometimes you need look no further than the village pond.

River carp are naturally attracted to weir pools, and are fun to catch wherever you fish. During filming for his TV series, when Go Fishing visited Spain and the mighty River Ebro, John located numbers of common carp running into double figures just off the main channel in a tiny, rocky overshoot pool. On freelined bread flake trundled around in the turbulence, bites were not slow in coming.

CHAPTER FOUR

TACKLE

DURING the 1980s more specialized tackle was marketed to feed the growing demand for carp fishing than for any other branch of fishing in the UK ever. Carp fishing has indeed become big business. Unfortunately, newcomers to the sport often suffer under the illusion that unless they are equipped with all the latest gadgetry they won't catch carp, which is simply not true.

RODS

Test curves

Rods designed and sold specifically for carp fishing usually have a 'test curve' rating printed along with the manufacturer's logo immediately above the handle. This provides a guide to the rod's power and therefore suggested line strengths to go with it so that both rod and line stretch in harmony like one enormous elastic band. To find out the suggested line strength for a particular rod you simply multiply its test curve rating by 5. For instance – a test curve of 2 lb will result in an ideal line strength of around 10 lb. It is as simple as that. To find the lower limit of lines that can safely be used with a rod, multiply by 4 (8 lb test) and by 6 for the upper limit (12 lb test).

These figures of course offer only a general guideline, because in experienced hands far lighter and heavier lines could be used in special circumstances with the same rod. But there has to be a better yardstick than judging the power of a rod purely by its looks, and as yet no one has improved on the test curve principle. Incidentally the words 'test curve' relate to the strain (in lbs) required to pull the rod's tip into a quarter circle, a method devised originally for rods made of built-cane which had an all-through progressive action.

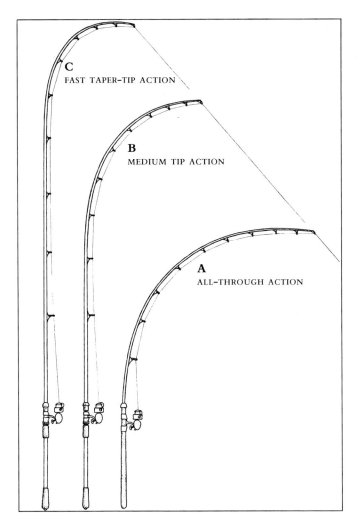

FIGURE 2 *Carp rod
actions*

Action

In addition to the rod's power, its action must also be considered. Most rods fall roughly into one of three popular categories. Rods which (similar to built-cane) bend progressively along their length, into a full curve under maximum load are described as *all-through action* ·(fig. 2A). Those whose action is mostly in the upper half or tip section are called *medium tip action* (fig. 2B). Rods where only the upper tip really bends to any degree are called *fast taper* (fig. 2C). All-through action rods are

For fishing at close range and for subduing large carp in overgrown parts of the fishery, rods with an all-through action are imperative. They absorb the fish's lunges, while the line stretches in complete harmony.

designed for close-in situations and for fishing at reasonably short range, say distances of up to 30/40 yd. Beyond this, for picking up the line and subsequently setting the hook when striking at greater distances, up to say 70/80 yd, a 'medium tip action' is the tool for the job. This is probably the most useful all-round actioned carp rod. To cope with still greater distances, 90 yd plus (far more specialized fishing), a fast taper-action rod is needed. However, because a fast taper rod bends very little other than in the extreme tip, you need to be especially careful not to rip out the hook or snap the line when bringing a heavy fish to the net on the end of a short line.

Nowadays, few carp rods are manufactured from either built-cane or fibre-glass. Carbon fibre, with various strengthening and shock absorbing agents added such as 'Kevlar', has more or less taken over the specialist market, resulting in rods of a very narrow profile which, in addition to being immensely strong, are pleasantly light to use. Rods by Daiwa, Ryobi, North Western Blanks, Tri Cast and Century Composites fall into this category.

Length

While two-piece 13 ft 'specials' are perhaps necessary for ultra-long-range carp fishing, most carp rods are produced in either 11 or 12 ft models. For picking up line at distance and for overall carp fishing into deep waters I would suggest that a 12-footer is absolutely ideal. For all close-range work, casting and playing fish beneath overhanging trees, fishing overgrown jungle-type swims, etc., the standard length of 11 ft is perfect. In fact an 11-footer with a test curve of somewhere between 1¼–2 lb (taking lines 8–10 lb test) is as close to the ideal rod as you could get.

A word at this point is perhaps in order about handle length, or more accurately where the screw reel fitting is positioned, because far too many rods have the reel fitting placed higher up the handle than is necessary. It may look very trendy, but what is the point in having a foot of rod sticking out beyond your elbow when playing a fish. Not only is the rod's effective length reduced by this amount, it

The ideal rod for striking the delicate bites of crucian carp and enjoying the fight they give, is a 13-ft match rod. Those designed with an 'easy' action for fishing the waggler are highly recommended.

is impossible to lay the rod over for applying sidestrain if the butt is so long it cannot be moved easily across your stomach. A good guide to the ideal distance is the length of a hand grip (at the bottom end) added to the length of your forearm and hand. The reel should then fit immediately below your hand. For the average adult this varies between 21 and 24 in from butt cap to reel stem – no more.

Rods for crucians

To the best of my knowledge there has never been a rod designed or marketed solely for the purpose of catching crucian carp. This is no doubt due to the market for such a rod being very small, coupled with the fact that any 12 or 13 ft match-come-float rod suitable for taking roach or bream is ideally suited to catching crucians.

REELS

The main requirement of any fixed-spool reel used for carp fishing is that it should have a wide spool so that the line comes off in large loose coils, as opposed to tight coils which restrict casting and bait presentation. Also, the spool should hold enough line, say 200 yd of 8/10 or 12 lb test mono. A super-fast retrieve is not required; I repeat – not required. The playing of fish is much smoother with a reel of standard gear ratio. A sensitive clutch, however, is of paramount importance if, like me, you prefer to play fish using the clutch.

In recent years the tactic of tightening the clutch right down and backwinding to play the fish through the gears instead of the clutch has been popularized by many specialist anglers. I would suggest, however, that by learning to use the clutch for the purpose it was designed for – by setting it properly so that the spool rotates and gives line before reaching full load – remains the most efficient way of ensuring that a big fish takes no more line than you actually need to give. And for controlling fish hooked close to, or actually right in among snaggy swims, this is very important.

You simply tighten the drag knob until line can just be pulled firmly yet smoothly from the spool – no more, no less. This of course prompts the question, which type of reel is best: reels with a standard front-adjusting clutch (built into the spool itself), as in the legendary Mitchell 300 and 400 range of reels; or the more recent skirted-spool, rear-drag reels, a format most manufacturers now seem to be producing. Unfortunately it is a question I cannot answer because the choice is a very personal one. I do in fact use both types. Skirted-spool reels do not allow line to slip down and become tangled between spool and the rotor housing; in addition, because the drag knob is situated at the rear or bottom of the reel, clutch adjustment even whilst playing a fish is found easier by the majority of fishermen. On the other hand, front drags are far less complicated; they have fewer parts to wear, and less torque on the system because only the spool turns and not the rotor.

In recent years many innovative creations have been added to fishing reels, including electronic wizardry, such as mini bite alarms which bleep and light up as the spool rotates and line is taken – though these have yet to catch on. Something that has become an important feature to carp anglers, however, in particular those presenting baits on heavy leaded shock or bolt rigs (see 'Bolt rig ledgering', p. 115) is the 'baitrunner' design patented by 'Shimano' which, through a trip lever, allows the spool to be completely disengaged from the drag system. Thus, a carp belting off is allowed to do so with the bale arm in the closed position as the spool rotates freely. There is even a separate 'spool drag' for when the baitrunner facility is in operation. Simply by turning the handle again the spool is returned to its pre-set drag and disengaged the baitrunner lever.

At the end of the day, you get what you pay for. So above all, invest in a good-quality reel, as opposed to one crammed with gimmicks. It should have a strong bale arm that incorporates a roller which actually rotates as the line pulls across it (to obviate excess friction), and it should be smooth in operation. Those which run on two or three sets of ball bearings, as do top-of-the-range models by ABU, Shimano, Ryobi, Mitchell and Daiwa, are highly recommended. For catching crucian carp, where close-range

fishing with much lighter lines is the order of the day,
choose a miniature fixed-spool with a super-sensitive
clutch or a centre pin. Both allow the fight of crucians to
be enjoyed to the full.

LINES

Contrary to all the advertising hype accompanying every
new line as it arrives on the market, very little has changed
with monofilament line during the last few decades. This is
possibly because it is, quite simply, a commodity which
can be developed no further. It is now as abrasion-
resistant, as fine and as supple, with a suitable degree of
stretch, as it is ever going to be. The plain truth is that if
you pre-stretch monofilament of a certain test and dia-

*When endeavouring to
catch heavy-weight
carp at close range,
such as this 27 lb
leather, do not put
your trust in a low-
stretch line. Thinner,
pre-stretched lines
have greatly reduced
elasticity and will part
when you most need a
shock absorber.*

meter, it will become that much thinner and therefore easier to fool the carp with. But at what price – and this is what everyone seems to forget – because it will then have greatly reduced elasticity, and it is the elastic-band action, or 'stretch', of regular monofilament that permits the landing of big fish on light lines.

Remove the 'buffer', as has happened with so-called revolutionary, much thinner lines (which have been reduced to minimal stretch) and the line parts just when you don't want it to: with the fish thumping away beneath the rod tip on a short line, about to be netted. It has been my experience as a tackle dealer, even after warning carp anglers of the consequences, that more have parted company with big fish hooked on low-diameter, pre-stretched lines than for any other reason.

Having said all this, low-diameter pre-stretched mono-filament does make excellent hook lengths. A thinner line tied to the hook is bound to encourage more bites, especially when presenting floaters or fishing in clear water. Only when fishing at extreme range, however, (100 yd plus) would I ever consider filling the reel with a pre-stretched line; and then only because regular mono, due to its inherent stretch, inhibits hook penetration on the strike.

I have for very many years relied upon Sylcast (in sorrel) and Maxima Chameleon for all my carp fishing. Both are consistently smooth, have just the right amount of stretch and are extremely supple. When I am winding new line straight on to the reel, I increase its suppleness by removing any coil caused by being stored on spools. This 'relaxing' process makes fishing with brand new line a pleasure instead of a nightmare because the 'spring' has been taken out. After filling up the spool and fixing the reel to the rod, thread the line through the rings and tie a large loop on the end. Slip it over a gate post or something similar and walk 30 yd away. Then wind gently down and slowly bend the rod into a full curve, holding it there for several seconds. Now point the rod at the fence post and wind until the line is tight to the reel with the rod straight. Walk slowly backwards a few paces 'feeling' just how much stretch there is in new monofilament. When it is really tight, obviously long before full elasticity is reached, hold it there for ten seconds. Afterwards, it can be wound back onto the spool nicely limp and ready for work. This may sound a bit of a rigmarole but I can assure you it is well worth the effort.

HOOK LENGTHS

In addition to using both regular and pre-stretched monofilament for the hook length, the suppleness of braided dacron makes it a fine alternative. In fact, all kinds of braided hook lengths are available to carp fishermen, from the standard black, low-stretch but incredibly supple braided dacron (also available camouflaged and flecked) to the multi-strands like Gamastrand floss and Kryston, both of which separate on the bottom into numerous gossamer single strands. The latter gives the carp greater confidence in accepting the bait with the advantage that the multi-strands return to one unit and full strength for striking and playing the fish.

HOOKS

Because it is the final link connecting you to what could be the carp of a lifetime, think seriously about the type and strength of hook when buying them. Never buy inexpensive hooks, or simply ask the tackle dealer for a packet of size 8 eyed hooks. In complete innocence he could be thinking of his customer's pocket and hand over cheapies which bend or spring open under minimal pressure. What you need is a hook that can be totally relied upon, forged with either a bronze or black finish, and chemically sharpened or etched to a needle point (keep a small stone handy for ensuring they stay sharp). My favourite hooks for heavy fishing are the Drennan super specialist and the Mustad 34021 O'Shaunessy patterns. In these I have complete confidence, whether cranking in a whopper from a jungle swim or taking it easy with medium-sized carp hooked in a completely snag-free environment.

For really light carping when stepping down to, say, 6 lb test for presenting floating baits to shy fish in clear

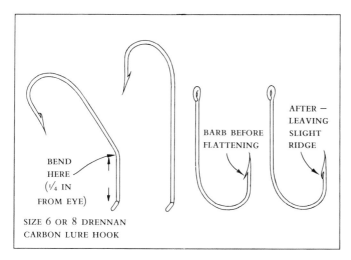

FIGURE 3 *Hooks*

BEND
HERE
(¼ IN
FROM EYE)

SIZE 6 OR 8 DRENNAN
CARBON LURE HOOK

BARB BEFORE
FLATTENING

AFTER —
LEAVING
SLIGHT
RIDGE

water, or going even lighter with a reel line of 2½ lb test tied direct to the hook for catching crucians, then the Drennan carbon specimen range fits the bill perfectly. In sizes 12 to 8 these particular hooks are fine enough in the wire not to inhibit carp from sucking up the bait, yet strong enough to stay in shape throughout a tough battle.

In recent years hook manufacturers have tried hard to stay in touch with current trends within carp fishing, one such development being 'the bent hook' (see fig. 3). Originally, a Drennan long-shank carbon lure (trout fishing) hook was bent inwards ¼ in down from the eye. Used in conjunction with a boilie presented on a hair/bolt rig, in consistent hooking terms this format is considered almost flawless. There are now several similar patterns of hooks (already bent) from which to choose, including the Drennan 'starpoint' and the 'Gardner' bent hook. For most situations in carp fishing, however, I still prefer to put my faith in a forged standard round-bend, medium-shank eyed hook whose point has been chemically etched to sharp perfection. I do, however, doctor the barb itself by flattening it with a pair of forceps to aid both penetration and subsequent removal (see fig. 3).

Always check each hook carefully before tying it on, which takes but a second. As with everything man-made, every so often you come across a duff one. In the case of a hook this means that it has not been properly tempered. Test each hook by putting the point beneath your thumb nail and try to lever it open.

For presenting many of the larger particle baits, and especially boilies, to crafty, well-educated carp the bolt rig is extremely effective. This modest-sized common carp accepted a side-hooked black-eyed bean and will come to no harm placed on a foam-lined unhooking mat.

It is often very much easier to unhook carp using long-nosed artery forceps. This young angler has sensibly kept his fish in the wet net and laid it upon a bed of soft grass well away from the gravel margins to remove the hook.

KNOTS

Poorly tied knots, and knots of poor design, are one of the main contributing factors to carp being lost. I still see references in articles and books to the 'five-turn half blood knot' as being a suitable knot for tying eyed hooks to catch big fish like carp. Yet this knot can so easily pull or fracture under the kind of pressures involved.

The knot I put complete faith in is called the mahseer knot, handed on to me by my guide, Suban, when after the legendary fish of that name in India. Its stength (see fig. 4A) lies in the fact that the end is trapped beneath two loops, instead of the standard half blood knots' one loop. For eyed hooks that are going to be used in the most demanding of situations the mahseer knot is unbeatable because it actually 'stretches' under full load instead of strangling the line.

With modern carbon hooks, which have particularly neat eyes, especially in the smaller sizes, the mahseer knot can prove rather bulky to tie. In this case, the seven-turn tucked half blood knot (see fig. 4B) is both quick and easy to tie.

Whilst both these knots are perfect for tying mono-filament, for dacron and other braids the choice lies between two more popular knots. The 'palomar knot' (see fig. 4C) is simple to tie and also creates minimal strangula-tion of the line. It is not an easy knot to manage with small-eyed hooks because the line has to be doubled into a loop and passed through the eye. Devised by the late Richard Walker and named after his son, the 'Grinner' knot (see fig. 4D) is far less constricting than the blood knots and technically more efficient because all five turns around the line are trapped against the eye, not just the end one.

Both of these knots are also good for tying multistrand floss, which is not the easiest material to deal with particularly if you work out of doors and suffer rough finger tips. However, provided you wet the length to be tied and keep it moist whilst bedding the knot down gently, both the palomar and the grinner work efficiently.

While the four previously described knots are all you will ever need for tying hooks and swivels on to the main

FIGURE 4 *Knots*

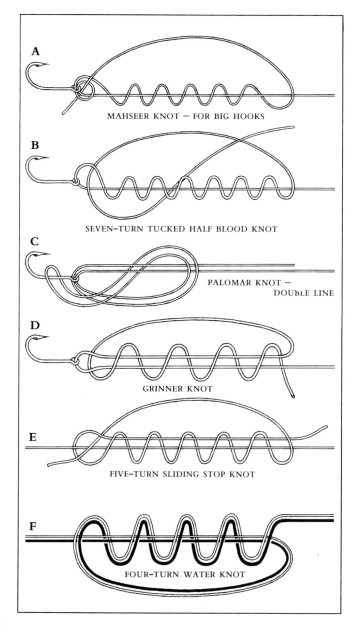

A

MAHSEER KNOT — FOR BIG HOOKS

B

SEVEN–TURN TUCKED HALF BLOOD KNOT

C

PALOMAR KNOT —
DOUBLE LINE

D

GRINNER KNOT

E

FIVE–TURN SLIDING STOP KNOT

F

FOUR–TURN WATER KNOT

line, or for hook and bomb links, etc., to cope with every demand in carp fishing there are two more valuable additions well worth learning to tie. The simple stop knot and the four-turn water knot. The stop knot (see fig. 4E) which can be moved up or down the line (always wet it first) is used in conjunction with a small bead as a stop against which the controller float rests when presenting floating baits. It can be tied with a short length of reel line or power gun which is softer and slides through the rod rings easily. Remember to leave the ends around 1½ in long so they 'fold' when the line passes back and forwards through the rod rings under the pressure of a fish being played.

The four-turn water knot (see fig. 4F) is great for joining a fixed-lead paternoster (of either heavier or lighter strain) to the main line. It has enormous advantages for joining two lines together where the only alternative is a swivel, which all too easily picks up debris and obviously weakens the rig because two extra knots are required. The four-turn water knot is quicker, neater, lighter and most importantly is stronger, because the main line is simply wound around and locked into the added link creating the minimum of constriction.

INDICATORS

Actually watching a carp suck the bait into its huge mouth is, of course, the best bite indication of all. It opens up a fascinating world of knowledge, making carp fun to take from the surface on floaters, especially when they can be observed at close range through really clear water approaching and finally accepting a freelined bait. A line snaking out across the surface is an exciting and most positive indication. In precious few situations (see Free-lining), however, can the line beyond the rod tip be regarded as the indicator to watch.

Coil indicators

Necessity calls for a visual indicator fixed between the butt ring and reel which is easily seen, easily attached, and which relates to both forward and drop-back bites. For years (some still do) anglers simply squeezed a piece of bread or a coil of silver kitchen foil, on to the line midway between butt ring and reel. Simple coil indicators (they can also be made from plastic piping in a variety of weights) are ideal for short freelining or ledgering sessions, especially

FIGURE 5 *Coil*
indicators

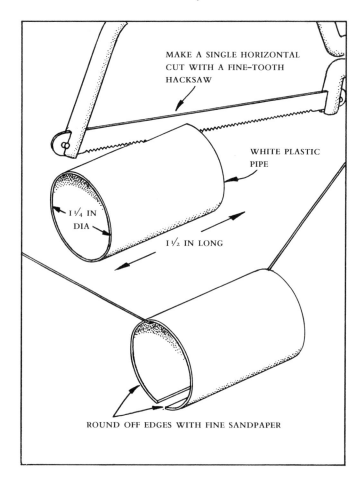

MAKE A SINGLE HORIZONTAL
CUT WITH A FINE-TOOTH
HACKSAW

WHITE PLASTIC
PIPE

1 1/4 IN
DIA

1 1/2 IN LONG

ROUND OFF EDGES WITH FINE SANDPAPER

for the wandering opportunist angler carrying the
minimum of tackle (see fig. 5).

Monkey climbers

The most popular of all carp indicators are, in effect,
'bobbins' on a stick which do not blow about in the wind.
They are available in a variety of weights to counteract
sub-surface tow and to indicate drop-back bites in certain
circumstances. If a certain amount of your carp fishing will
take place during darkness or in poor light, choose a
monkey with a clear body that will accept a luminous
betalight element (see fig. 6). Otherwise, go for bright
daytime colours like yellow or orange. Monkeys which
run super freely on a black (PTFE-coated) stick, aptly

Having pre-baited a shallow bar along the opposite bank, the angler waits patiently for a run. The rods are supported on a 'rod pod' frame specially designed for banks of hard gravel. These allow the entire set-up, including bank sticks, bite alarms and monkey climbers, to be moved easily as one unit.

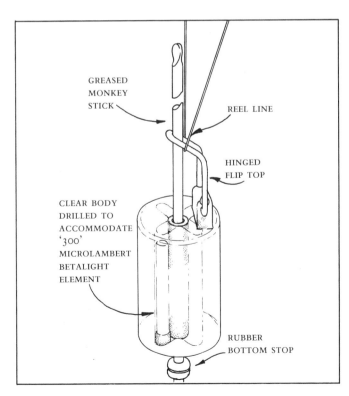

GREASED
MONKEY
STICK

REEL LINE

HINGED
FLIP TOP

CLEAR BODY
DRILLED TO
ACCOMMODATE
'300'
MICROLAMBERT
BETALIGHT
ELEMENT

RUBBER
BOTTOM STOP

FIGURE 6 *Monkey climbers*

called 'grease monkeys', are worth the extra money as the
body slides up and down effortlessly.

Bite alarms/buzzers

While monkey climbers work perfectly well without any
electrical help in registering a bite when ledgering, they are
used almost exclusively in conjunction with an electric bite
alarm or, as they are affectionately known, a 'buzzer'.
Buzzers have now become synonymous with carp fishing
almost to the point that some carp fishermen would feel
distinctly 'undressed' without them. This is a pity because
the substitution of gadgetry for technique rather limits
enjoyment.

Antenna-type buzzers

These, the first design in buzzers ever marketed, are still
popular because they fit nicely into the lower price bracket
and work on the contact-breaker principle. When the line
is pulled across the antenna, at the bottom of which is a

FIGURE 7 *Antenna-
type buzzers*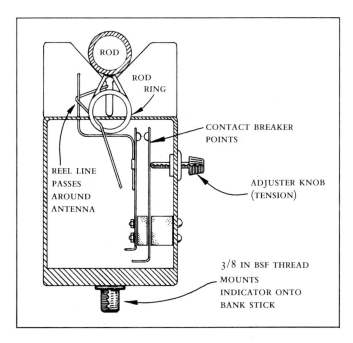

breaker point, contact is made and the buzzer sounds in conjunction with a light-emitting diode for visual warning (see fig. 7).

The antenna can be tensioned or relaxed as required for registering twitches or steady pulls by simple knob adjustment. This type of buzzer, however, is capable of registering only a short or a continuous (so long as the carp keeps swimming away) bite. It cannot relate to the speed at which line is being taken.

Optonic bite indicators

These particular buzzer-alarms, which are in fact now almost standard gear amongst carp enthusiasts, also indicate the speed at which line is being taken off the reel. For every ¾ in of line which travels across the sensitive 'wheel' a single bleep tone plus warning light is emitted, so you can instantly relate to the kind of bite, whether it is a mere twitch, a slow run, or a scorching run. As the line rotates the wheel a tiny fan blade spigoted to the wheel with a fine spindle interupts the light beam of a mini photo electric cell.

This system is available in various self-contained cordless compact forms, with or without volume and tone control, and with sensors (or heads) connected by wires to a sounder box which can be positioned several yards away inside a bivi so it effectively becomes an alarm clock. Unfortunately some are even louder than alarm clocks. Another feature available on some models is a green latching light which stays on for 10 seconds (after the bite) to show you on which rod the buzzer indicated should you not have noticed.

The Magnetronic is a new concept from Optonic which looks and works in the same way, but uses a magnet and reed switch in conjunction with the wheel instead of a photo-electric cell. It only drains the standard PP3 battery when the line moves and is noticeably more rain resistant than all previous models.

All electronic bite alarms naturally become the front rod rest heads, for which the 'buzzer bar' was invented. Available in alloy or stainless steel there are buzzer bars to take two, three or even four rods (stick with two) which

Surrounded by the beauty and natural history of a secluded lake, the angler can allow his eyes and mind to wander away from the rods, knowing that the slightest movement of the line will register in a series of bleeps from the Optonic bite indicators.

simply screw into the standard bank-stick thread. For both front and back rests (separate U-type screw-in heads take the rod butts) invest in a pair of telescopic bank sticks to allow for a variety of different marginal levels.

For the really hard banking of some gravel pits, reservoirs and the like, the rod pod is the answer. This is a complete rod set-up with a ground frame combining bank sticks and twin buzzer bars with an aerial bar located in the middle to take monkey climbers. It saves having to crunch about, ramming or hammering in bank sticks which can only distract from the fishing and even spoil the enjoyment and solitude of other anglers close by.

FLOATS

The float of course, is the oldest indicator of them all. And while today's youngsters, through no fault of their own, may well come straight into the carp fishing scene and immediately start to rely on electronic bite alarms coupled

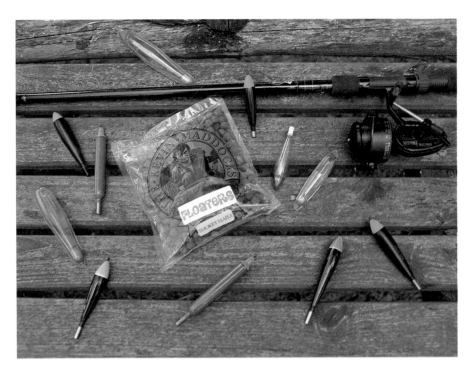

to bolt-rig ledgering set-ups, float fishing will always be available as an art to learn.

There is nothing more exciting than crouching down in the marginal growth holding the rod in anticipation when less than 5 yd out amongst a huge patch of feeding bubbles the float tip suddenly pops upwards and keels right over in a perfect 'lift' bite. Carp do not warrant a super-sensitive range of floats, as do dace or roach. Plain peacock quill cut into suitable lengths, with the herl removed from the stem and the tip painted with ½ in of fluorescent orange or red, is quite adequate. I never bother with eyes or rings at the bottom because threading the line through these could be suicidal should a carp wind its way through heavy weed. In that situation, I want the float to come free instantly, and all I have lost is a few pence. The float is usually fixed at the bottom end only (see 'Float fishing') with a wide section of silicon float rubber. By all means use commercial wagglers or bodied peacock wagglers, but always attach them with silicon tubing as opposed to the eye and 'locking shot' method, because with the list method all shots need to be close to the bait.

For presenting all floating baits, from tiny cat biscuits to a large chunk of bread crust, any further than a few yards, use a loaded floating controller. They are available in a variety of shapes and sizes.

FLOATING CONTROLLERS

Available in all sorts of shapes and sizes, the controller is an indispensible piece of equipment for presenting both small and large floaters to surface-feeding carp. It has a swivel at the top, plus a coloured tip for good visual location at distance, plus a weighted stem so it sits vertically in the surface film.

Controllers originated from the age-old spherical bubble float made from clear plastic, into which water could be put to aid casting. However, striking with bubble floats causes so much water displacement that much of the power never reaches the hook. It was for this reason, unhappy with commercially-produced controllers at that time (now there are several good designs), that I devised my 'Ten-pin' which, as its name implies, is shaped exactly like a bowling pin. Rounded and wide at the top, into which a size 10 Berkeley swivel is glued, it tapers down to a narrow wrist which consists of a weighted stem of brass, plugged into the balsa body. I required a weighted surface controller that could be flipped even underarm from banks suffering badly from overhead branches, up to distances of 30 yd or more. I am pleased to say even the small 'Ten-pin' (there are two sizes) accomplishes this with ease (see Floater fishing).

SUNDRIES

Landing-nets

Traditionally, carp landing-nets have always been triangular in shape with two arms supported in a preformed spreader block, fitted with a standard BSF ⅜th thread for screwing into any landing-net pole, whether single stem or telescopic. A nylon cord stretched between the tip of each end keeps them slightly bowed, and thus the whole frame remains reasonably rigid. For several years I have used the North Western specimen net, which has strong, hollow fibre-glass arms and is available in 36 in, 42 in and 50 in sizes. Frankly, having easily slipped two pike each of exactly 50 in long (one a 30-pounder) into the 42 in carp model, I cannot see why anything larger, with its associated awkward manoeuvrability (especially in dense undergrowth), is ever required for carp, taking into account that carp are considerably shorter for their weight than pike.

For 'stalking' carp, I much prefer to carry a smaller net: 24 in diameter, round frame fixed with a 24 in deep twin mesh net, micro at the base with minnow mesh sides. The junction where the screw thread joins the telescopic pole needs to be supported when hoisting out a heavy weight or the frame will collapse, nevertheless this is certainly worth the trouble for the net's portability. I have in fact landed several fish (up to 26¾ lb) with the telescopic pole fully extended and these could not have been netted with a larger, heavier, less manoeuvrable triangle framed net: for example, carp which have become stuck fast on the surface wrapped around lily stems, or which are simply lying there exhausted on the surface immovable in beds of thick soft weeds, tantalizingly beyond the reach of the larger specimen net's single pole. Whichever frame you decide upon (perhaps for overall use, a triangular 36 in model is best) ensure that the net has a micro or soft nylon base (as used in carp sacks) and that the wall mesh is soft and knotless. Twin meshes are extremely popular, and rightly so. The larger wall mesh allows the net to be steered easily through the water, while the soft nylon or micro bottom ensures that the carp's body mucus remains intact and that the terminal rig does not become entangled.

Sacks

If you can take a photo of your carp immediately after capture, it's best not to retain it. Simply leave it in the landing-net (even before unhooking) in the margins while the camera is adjusted and a suitable spot found where the light is even and not full of shadows. Then even self-photography with the aid of an air-release cable can be accomplished quickly and with minimum inconvenience to the carp.

As carp live a long life, and in popular fisheries will no doubt be caught dozens, perhaps even hundreds of times,

For many situations, particularly when stalking modest-sized carp in overgrown waters, a 24 in diameter, round landing-net frame fitted with a deep, twin-mesh net, is infinitely more manouvreable than a giant triangular model. A round net can easily handle fish up to 20 lb.

you owe it to the carp and to the angler after you to return the fish without harm. This entails retaining it in a soft nylon sack of adequate proportions. Sacks punched with numerous holes for the water to pass freely through are highly recommended. They come in various sizes (4 × 5 ft is ideal) with a draw-string top or long zip, and are black in colour which helps keep the carp quiet inside. Remember always to fully soak the sack before putting the carp inside, or some of the carp's valuable body mucus will be removed, leaving it vulnerable to parasites and disease. Select a quiet shaded spot away from full sunlight and tie the retaining cord tightly to a bankside branch. Where none exist, I push my long-nosed forceps into the bank and tie the cord to them. Ensure that the carp has at least 18 in of water so it can fully submerge, and once again retain it for the shortest period of time only. Lastly never put more than one carp into one sack.

Unhooking mats

For the safe removal of hooks – safe that is for the carp, which can all too easily flap up and down on gravel banking and scrape itself raw – unhooking mats have been

*Though large,
specialized weigh
slings and bags are
available, and perhaps
necessary for really
monstrous fish, most
carp are weighed with
less fuss and certainly
less stress by un-
screwing the landing-
net top and hooking it
directly on to the
scales, remembering to
deduct the net's weight
afterwards.*

designed. For gravel pit fisheries in particular, renowned for stony banks which never grass over, these foam-filled unhooking mats are an absolute must for ensuring that the fish goes back in to the water in the condition it came out. At a pinch, an old square of carpet underlay or piece of $1/2$ in thick dense foam will suffice. Remember, however, to dampen whatever you use so the body mucus is not disturbed.

Weighing carp/slings

Continuing the theme of disturbing the fish's condition as little as possible, it's just as easy to unscrew the landing-net top and hoist it on to the scales complete with carp to weigh it, remembering to deduct the net's weight afterwards, as to remove the carp to weigh it. Should this prove impossible, have a large pre-wetted, soft nylon sling handy into which the carp can be gently moved immediately after unhooking. After weighing, take the sling into the water and allow the carp to swim out under its own steam. This is also a good time for that final 'returning' photo.

CHAPTER FIVE

BAITS

FROM the vast majority of what is written today about carp baits the newcomer could easily be led into thinking that only designer boilies concocted from a high nutritional value protein mix and flavoured with exotic essences or oils from the far east will catch carp. This, of course, is not true.

Carp derive nutritional value from almost any food source and can be caught on a whole variety of baits, not just boilies. In fact I cannot think of any bait apart from a spinner (even these account for the odd carp) which carp will not readily accept.

What must be accepted, however, is that the more times they are caught on a particular kind, type, flavour, shape or even size of bait, the more suspicious they naturally become. So that, and this applies especially to carp in hard-fished waters, eventually they learn to refuse all the more commonly used baits that have fooled them in the past – baits like bread in all its forms, sweetcorn, luncheon meat, simple pastes and so on. The answer is to find new baits that they will eagerly accept. To stay catching, you need to be forever ringing the changes, switching from one bait to another once the bulk of the carp you are after start to wise up. It is always worthwhile baiting up with a new offering whilst still catching them with the old bait, before its effectiveness wears out.

All this is not to say that even carp from waters where they have seen every bait before will not accept a much used bait under the right circumstances, presented either differently or in a spot the carp have never learnt to associate with danger. The record carp of 51 lb 6 oz caught by Chris Yates from famous Redmire pool in 1980, for instance, sucked up what was then a much used bait, namely sweetcorn. And more than any other fishery in the country, Redmire's carp have seen every new bait ever invented, but this did not stop Chris using sweetcorn effectively, presented beneath a float, too. The secret is to

Manufactured carp baits have certainly come a long way. The prepacked ingredients available from most specialist tackle shops allow you to enjoy an absorbing side hobby by concocting your own designer baits.

keep an open mind on the subject of bait and through observation, trial and error, combined with the experiences of other anglers fishing the same water, try various types of bait until runs occur on a regular basis. Do not ever run away with the idea that there is a magic bait, one to catch carp from wherever you fish, because such a bait doesn't exist.

Learn to use a whole variety of baits, and experience will teach you where each is applicable. Don't sit there with a lump of bread flake on the hook when all the carp in the lake grew wise to bread and lost their interest in it 10 years ago. Several sessions using a particular bait without a run should help the penny drop. By the same token, don't go in with a 12-bore to shoot a sparrow. In other words don't spend a fortune on the latest-flavoured boilies to catch carp which have only recently been introduced into a lake, or have seen little prior attention from anglers. In both cases, it's well worth keeping something in reserve while experimenting with far cheaper and more commonly used baits.

This is not a cookery book, and you will not find a whole list of recipes for making different-flavoured and

different-structured boilies, as good and effective a bait as they are. And make no mistake about it, boilies are a fine bait – the most effective carp bait ever devised. However, the boilie is just one type of bait amongst dozens. Besides, tackle shops sell a wide enough choice of manufactured boiled baits, in terms of colour, size and flavours, shelf life and frozen, without my repeating them all. I am going to take you back through the history of carp fishing baits by providing a comprehensive list of exactly what can be used to catch carp.

Don't just stick to luncheon meat. The variety of tinned and sausage type meats available from the local delicatessen or supermarket is enormous. They can be cut into oblongs or cubes with a thin, long-bladed knife.

MANUFACTURED BAITS

Bread

Bread can be used in several ways, either new, as '*flake*' compressed onto the hook, *crust* fished on the surface, or the inside of the loaf (one several days old is best) kneaded with water into a *paste*. To this paste various flavourings and colourings may be added: *custard powder* which turns it yellow; *aniseed* which really makes it smell; *marmite* or *Bovril* to give it a savoury smell; *grated cheese* to pep it up (a great chub and barbel bait this); and so on. Bread has many possibilities. I once asked a friend who is a baker to bake me half a dozen loaves dyed black with powder colouring, because the carp I was after at the time were scared by the whiteness of ordinary bread. And very effective the *black flake* and *black crusts* proved too. Plain white flake, however, is one of the best crucian baits around.

Cheese

Cut into *small cubes* cheese can be fished on a hair rig (see 'Ledgering' p. 116), or simply freelined (p. 88), float-fished (p. 91), or presented on a standard ledger rig (p. 112). There are countless textures and flavours to try. Plain ordinary *processed cheese* sold from large blocks is probably the nicest to use. The smelly, crumbly ones, like *Danish Blue* or *Gorgonzola* are best mixed into a stiff paste with equal quantities of bread paste. There is lots to experiment with here.

Meats

A tin of *luncheon meat* should always be kept in the back of the car or in the tackle bag as a standby. It is a sound investment. Cut into cubes (no longer than the hook shank) luncheon meat will catch carp from anywhere. *Stuffed pork roll*, tinned *ham*, and *spam* are also worth trying. Or what about all those spicey sausages in skins like *garlic sausage*, or *black pudding* made largely from pigs' blood; they are all fabulous carp attractors which, when cut into cubes, offer an endless variety of baits. The trouble is that you can't stop eating them, as all luncheon meat fans know only too well. Fresh meats are effective too, especially *liver*, either pigs' or calves' liver, carefully cut into squares and used like luncheon meat straight on the hook, or on a hair rig (p. 116). *Raw steak* shares with liver a high blood content which is particularly attractive to carp. It too should be cut into squares with a sharp knife, and, because of its stringy consistency, presented on a hair.

Tinned sausages like chipolatas cut into segments make great baits, as do both *pork* or *beef sausages* that have been cooked and left to cool, because then they can be cut into squares or oblongs.

Pork or beef *sausage meat* makes a fine paste. Simply keep adding flour whilst kneading until the stickiness disappears, leaving a firm hook bait which can be easily moulded.

Liver sausage, although expensive, kneads into a lovely smooth paste with cornflour added to stiffen it. Add a drop or two of brown liquid colouring if you think it is too light.

Tinned cat foods are available in dozens of different flavours which potentially all make excellent paste baits. Stiffen with cornflour and some wheatgerm until firm enough, and then test in a glass of water to see how long it will last without disintegrating. Add a small quantity of wheat gluten to act as a binder in brands which are difficult to work with.

PELLET FEED

By far the most effective bait available in pellet form – manufactured in various sizes from fry crumb to $\frac{1}{2}$ in diameter holding pellets – are those produced for the sole purpose of rearing trout and salmon. Formulated in various proportions of fish meal, oils and binders, *trout pellets* are effective as a surface attractor in their floating form, and as a sinking loose-feed crumb in the smallest sinking size. *Salmon fry crumb*, which have a higher oily fish content and are much darker in colour are especially good.

To convert this effective bait into a paste, put into a bowl and wet (without oversoaking) with hot water. Leave for 30 minutes to allow all the water to be absorbed, and then knead into a stiff paste adding cornflour to blot up any excess water. For added attraction (although these pellets are a complete food in themselves) Bovril, marmite, or Phillips yeast mixture (a bird tonic) may be mixed into the paste, which can then be popped into a polybag and put in the freezer for later use.

Pig pellets may also be kneaded into an aromatic paste to

good effect by following the same procedure. In fact all animal pellet food is worth experimenting with as potential carp baits. Those which do not hold together well are improved with the addition of beaten eggs to bind the mixture together plus cornflour or wheat gluten to stiffen it.

DRIED MILK PASTES

Coloured pastes with a rubbery texture guaranteed to withstand the attentions of small, nuisance species, are easily made from a mixture of dried milk derivatives, wheatgerm, flavouring and powder dye mixed with water.

Some of the richest derivatives to be extracted from milk make very effective paste baits. There are so many recipes this book could not contain them all, so here is a basic formula. Mix dry in a bowl one part of Casilan (from chemists) or calcium calcinate to two parts of Beemax (also from chemists) or plain wheatgerm. Then add sufficient water to which liquid or powder colour, plus a flavour, has been added and knead into a soft paste. The resulting paste will be rather sticky and rubbery, which makes it almost impervious to the pecking attentions of small unwanted nuisance species. Contrary to popular belief, this bait can be frozen for later use.

PARTICLE BAITS

These work effectively because much of the carp's natural daily diet consists of tiny particles of food sucked up individually over a wide area (see 'Feeding') as opposed to large concentrated food items.

Hempseed is the most effective particle of all, especially as an attractor because it really gets carp rooting about and holds them within a given area. Though it is individually too small to put on to a carp hook it can be threaded on to a fine hair stringer and tied in at the eye of the hook (fig. 8). Alternatively, and this is my preference, simply pre-bait or loose feed with stewed hempseed and on the hook use a larger particle. I once thought that only other small, darkish seeds or peas really worked in conjunction with hemp and in certain situations this still holds true, but when carp are really going potty on hempseed and chewing the bottom up, almost anything on the hook will produce a bite.

Dari seed is another small seed which like hemp is a fine attractor and is best presented several seeds at a time on a hair stringer (fig. 8).

The colourful array of baits shown here, most of which are available either pre-cooked in tins or in dried form, represent just a small selection of the particle baits which will catch carp. Use your imagination.

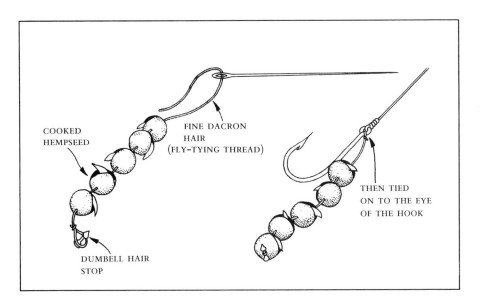

COOKED HEMPSEED

FINE DACRON HAIR (FLY-TYING THREAD)

THEN TIED ON TO THE EYE OF THE HOOK

DUMBELL HAIR STOP

FIGURE 8 *Threading hempseed onto a hair stringer*

Maple peas are an excellent hook bait used together with attractors like hemp, tares, or daris, or simply by itself as bait and attractor.

Tic beans are not unlike maples but are larger, heavier and work in the same way. They are a much under-rated carp bait.

Tares are only slightly larger than hemp (after stewing). They work effectively as both hook bait (on a hair stringer, fig. 8) and smelly attractors if left to stew in their own juices for a few days.

Wheat, once stewed, has a lovely nutty smell and is a really effective yet seldom-used, inexpensive particle bait. It is large enough to be fished two up on the hook, or threaded on to a hair. When its effectiveness starts to wane it can even be coloured by adding powder dye to the stewing water. Red and orange are favourites. The addition of a flavour might also help – try aniseed.

Maize needs to be pre-soaked for two days in hot water and then pressure cooked for 20 minutes, otherwise it appears too hard to use as bait. The prepared grain swells to twice its size, not unlike a giant but brighter grain of wheat (one grain to a size 8 hook is ideal). It is always much harder than wheat, however, and thus impervious to the attentions of small fish. Like wheat, it too may be coloured and flavoured although part of its secret is, I am sure, the pungent, nutty smell.

Sweetcorn is probably the most successful particle bait of all time, though its effectiveness soon wears off when everybody starts using it. It is, of course, a hybrid of the maize plant. Harvested while still soft, young and sweet, and not left to dry on the cob, its life may be extended as a bait on waters where carp have become suspicious of this 'yellow peril' by dyeing it with a powder colour mixed into a little hot water. Bright red or purple sweetcorn looks terrific and catches well. It is always worth keeping a tin or two in the tackle bag or boot of the car for catching crucian carp alone.

Peanuts are much loved by carp, and providing they are prepared properly will, contrary to popular belief, do the fish no harm. Put them into a tub with a rip-off lid, with plenty of space to spare. Cover by at least several inches of boiling water, to allow the nuts to expand fully. Fix the lid on tightly and leave for two days. Drain the excess water off and the nuts are ready for immediate use – or pop into polybags and into the freezer.

Standard-sized, ready-shelled nuts may be purchased reasonably cheaply from pet shops by the lb or in bulk. These are ideal for pre-baiting and loose feed. The much larger (and more expensive) jumbo-sized American pea-nuts make fabulous hook baits, one being nicely matched to a size 6 or 4 hook, and nicked on gently (side hooked) through either end leaving the point and barb well exposed. Two nuts are best threaded on to a hair.

Possessing tremendous inherent buoyancy, peanuts are great for fishing over and into thick weed. They tend to rest on top and remain visible to patrolling carp, unlike heavier particles which fall through and become hidden. Used over a bed of hempseed, American peanuts are a deadly bait whether float-fished (p. 91) or ledgered on a bolt rig (p. 117).

You must prepare *tiger nuts* in exactly the same way as maize or they cannot be used as bait. They are in fact a vegetarian food (available from health food shops) with a delightful crunchy, nutty flavour, for which carp also share a liking. To get carp really on to tigers may take several pre-baiting sessions, but once they have learnt to appreciate them, expect some fast action. Like peanuts they stay on well, and so can be reliably cast long distances. Tigers are also a great marginal bait. I present

To prepare extremely hard particles for carp baits, such as maize or the tiger nuts shown here, pre-soak for 2 days in cold water prior to pressure cooking for 20 minutes.

them two up on a size 4 hook beneath a length of peacock quill lift style (p. 94).

Black eyed beans are a rather bland salad bean. With its distinctive black eye, it catches well and is most versatile. It is cheap to buy in dry form from health food shops (or in tins already cooked), and may be prepared to your (or the carp's) liking. Stew as for peanuts adding colour and flavour as required. My favourite colours are dark red, brown, or orange, flavoured with caramel or butterscotch, but of course the permutations are endless. Present one on a size 8, two on a size 4 directly on to the hook, leaving the point and barb clear or thread on to a hair (fig. 8).

Chick peas. This round salad favourite, another excellent alternative for ringing the changes, is prepared, coloured and flavoured in exactly the same way as black eyes, or purchased pre-cooked in tins.

Butter beans. These flattish beans, largest by far of the particles, are tailor-made for fishing over dense weed-beds or thick silt. They are available uncoloured and pre-cooked in tins or may be purchased dry and then stewed, coloured and flavoured as all the other beans. Their size obviously permits the use of large hooks and even a single butter bean is heavy enough to freeline (p. 88) provided you cast gently.

Red kidney beans. If like me you adore 'Chili con carne', then this large, dark purple bean is no stranger. Carp love them too, whether presented over a bed of smaller attractors such as hemp or tares, or just as they are. As they need neither colour nor flavouring, simply buy them pre-cooked in tins and strain off the juices. Hook sizes 6 to 4 are ideal. To economize for regular pre-baiting, they can be purchased in bulk from health food shops and prepared in the same way as peanuts. Never be tempted to chew these beans unless they have been well stewed.

Borlotti beans also have the convenience of being available ready-cooked in a tin. Dark red in colour and slightly larger than a baked bean, individual beans should be side-hooked on a size 8 hook or presented on a hair two or even three up. Loose feed and pre-bait with the same, or use over an attractor such as hempseed.

Haricot beans. This, the most consumed bean of all when cooked in tomato sauce, is another 'change' particle bait. Buy tins of baked beans and drain off the sauce if you prefer them ready coloured, or buy a tin of plain haricot beans. One on a size 10 or two on an 8 does nicely.

NATURALS

Large quantities of stretched, dead maggots are sometimes the unfortunate result of heatwave conditions, when the tackle dealers' refrigeration units cannot cope with the warmth that the maggots generate. However, they can be put to good use for pre-baiting, and quickly turn carp into a feeding frenzy.

Maggots

These are without question as effective for catching carp (including crucians) as they are for most other species. And in the vast majority of fisheries this is the problem – maggots are not selective enough. Everything from a plump gudgeon upwards has not the slightest problem with even four maggots on a size 10 hook. There are two ways of dealing with this problem. Use maggots only in waters where carp are the dominant species. Or put so many in that when the nuisance fish become full up the carp move in and start pulling the bottom apart. Funnily enough, such a feeding pattern is induced whenever the fridge packs up in my tackle shop (usually in heatwave conditions), because dozens of gallons of 'stretched' maggots get tossed into the carp lake nearest the house. And wherever that spot happens to be, within an hour or two it is turned into a churning, bubbling, muddy mass of carp feeding with real abandon, their tails wavering across the surface as they skim along on their noses hoovering up the sudden food mass.

FIGURE 9 *Hair-rigged casters*

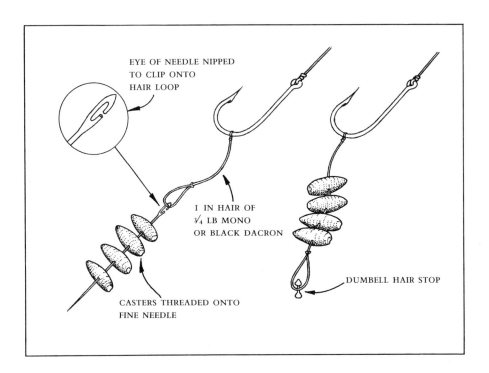

EYE OF NEEDLE NIPPED
TO CLIP ONTO
HAIR LOOP

I IN HAIR OF
¼ LB MONO
OR BLACK DACRON

CASTERS THREADED ONTO
FINE NEEDLE

DUMBELL HAIR STOP

Casters

Casters share the same pulling power as maggots for both nuisance species and carp, with the added benefit that they do not burrow into the silt or dense weed and become invisible. So in effect you need far less for loose feed. Carp also love floating casters, but to present them delicately without numerous refusals unusually light terminal tackle needs to be employed. Alternatively, they can be presented on a long hair, two, three or four up (fig. 9).

Worms

With the availability nowadays of so many manufactured baits, the poor old *worm* does not rate much of a look in. Considering that worms are free, this is a great pity because they are extremely effective carp baits. Use brandlings individually topped with a grain of corn, or two brandlings on a size 12 for crucian carp.

Larger carp always accept bunches of brandlings readily,

FIGURE 10 *Air-injected lobworm*

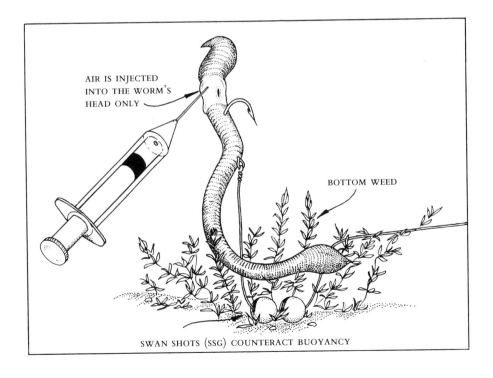

AIR IS INJECTED
INTO THE WORM'S
HEAD ONLY

BOTTOM WEED

SWAN SHOTS (SSG) COUNTERACT BUOYANCY

especially when they are rooting in silt and preoccupied with blood worms, while a large gyrating lobworm brings out that natural, animal aggression. Simply freeline (p. 88) on a size 6, or present beneath a float (p. 91), laid well on the bottom with a single shot 10 in from the hook. In really thick bottom weed, inject the head of the lob with a little air from a hypodermic syringe so it floats tantalizingly above the weed, using a swan shot or two to compensate for its buoyancy (fig. 10).

Shrimps/prawns

The most convenient way of buying these super baits is ready boiled, peeled and frozen from the local super-market. They may also be coloured. However, owing to their natural shellfish flavour, offering them just as they are usually produces action, even from particularly difficult carp. Pre-baiting works wonders, using at least 1 pint for every session.

Cockles

Cockles are also best purchased having been first boiled and de-shelled. Fishmongers sell them in bulk, enabling a batch to be split up into several polybags and popped into the freezer for later use. As with prawns, pre-baiting produces the goods and this necessitates introducing 1 pint or so into the swim for several consecutive days before actually fishing. Due to their bland taste, cockles are ideal for experimenting with flavours. Have a go at colouring them too. Use bright pink, red or orange powder dye – the results are staggering.

Mussels

Generally speaking freshwater mussels, and in particular the largest – the well-known swan mussel – seem to grow best of all in rich silty waters, be they estate lakes, ponds or pits. They can easily be gathered by pulling a long-handled garden rake along the bottom of the margins, and kept in a

An old-hat bait it may well be, and like as not most modern carp fishermen will probably not have used the succulent orange meat found inside the swan mussel. However it's free, it can be gathered from the lake margins, and is a part of the carp's natural diet.

bucket of water for a few days. To open the clam-like shell, use a thin-bladed knife to sever the powerful hinges holding the two halves together. This reveals the orange meat inside – a food source which carp almost everywhere will relish. A large chunk on a size 2 or 4 hook provides a fabulous bait, while the leftovers plus the insides from several other large mussels provides an attractive ground bait. Pre-baiting a swim every other day with the insides of 20 swan mussels could well provoke even difficult, well-fished carp that have seen all the regular pre-made baits, into a feeding frenzy. Try it and see. You do not need to use heavy leads or a bolt-rig set up for this approach. All you need to do is freeline (p. 88) the mussel meat and wait for the line to start peeling steadily from the spool in a confident run.

FLOATERS

Breadcrust

On heavily fished waters floating crust is considered to be
very old hat, and thus an ineffective bait for carp.
Nevertheless, it still has pulling power and will catch in
new fisheries and in fast, well-stocked carp waters where
competition for food among the fish is always high. Use
the tough crusts cut from either a white tin loaf or French
bread.

Pedigree chum mixers

These, the most popular and certainly the most versatile of
floating carp baits, can also be coloured and flavoured in
addition to using them straight from the box. Being small
and square, they catapult well, are relatively cheap if
purchased in bulk (3.5 kg bags), and fairly impervious to
the attentions of small nuisance fish. To prepare mixers for
hooking, hold a double handful under the tap so they are
all wet and pop straight into a polybag. Twenty minutes
later they will have absorbed the moisture, and will be easy
to hook without disintegrating whether you side-hook
one, or thread two or three on to a floating hair rig (see
'Floater fishing', p. 101).

My favourite way of 'doctoring' mixers is to gently heat
a batch for a couple of minutes in a frying pan containing a
liberal covering of garlic butter. And there are countless
permutations for spicing them up once carp noticeably
become suspicious of them in their plain form. Experiment
and have some fun.

Cat biscuits

Cat biscuits also make wonderful floaters for carp. They
come in all sorts of shapes too, ovals, stars, rounds, even
mini fish shapes. Pet food supply stores offer them in bulk
in both meat and fishy flavours. Prepare in exactly the
same way as 'mixers' for easy hooking.

Sunflower seeds

Sunflower seeds, which require soaking for a few hours for ease of hooking, are perhaps an unusual but nonetheless effective floater, possibly due to their high oil content. Whenever I sweep out the cockatiel aviary and dump the entire mess of loose seeds on to the surface of the lake closest to the house, the carp are up on the top and mopping them up post haste. Only soak those required for hook baits.

Boilies

Floating boilies are a bait which small, unwanted species like rudd and roach cannot peck to bits, and as such are the most selective of all floaters, whether side-hooked or presented on a hair.

Offer just one large (18–20 mm) boilie, which really stands out amongst a scattering of small attractor floaters such as cat biscuits or chum mixers; or a floating boilie of any size amongst a small scattering of others of the identical colour and size (see 'Floater fishing', p. 101).

If you cannot find pre-made floaters in the tackle shop of the size, colour and flavour desired, simply put a batch of regular, sinking boilies into a shallow baking tray and pop into a pre-heated oven for a few minutes. They should all then float. Experiment to make perfect.

BOILED BAITS (BOILIES)

I have purposefully left boiled baits, or 'boilies' as they are affectionately known, until the end of this chapter. They are not the panacea for catching carp easily that certain bait manufacturers would have us believe. However, boilies are extremely effective, and are a most selective bait for carp because nuisance species cannot deal with them. Either their pharyngeal teeth are not powerful enough to crush the outer skin enabling the soft insides to be swallowed (which is the whole idea of wrapping a

Baits for catching carp off the surface are cheap, readily avail-able and easily cata-pulted.

protective skin around the bait), or their mouths are simply too small.

It is said that there is nothing new in fishing and at times this fact is really brought home. For instance, one of the most famous carp baits of yesteryear, though seldom used nowadays – par-boiled potatoes – was in reality nothing less than a boilie years ahead of its time. But then, huge paste baits made from millet flour and boiled to enhance the natural gluten so as to make the surface rubbery and thus impervious to unwanted species, were concocted in India at least 100 years ago by those who sought the legendary mahseer. And now anyone can walk into even a non-specialist tackle shop and be spoilt for choice by the sheer amount of varying sizes, colours and flavours of boiled baits on offer, both frozen and shelf life.

Shelf-life boilies are certainly the most convenient of manufactured baits. You simply need to choose a size from minis up to gob-stopper, 20 mm ones, select a flavour and colour which hasn't seen much use on the water in question, and give them a try. There is no wonder flavour or magic boilie, so don't waste your time looking for one.

Consider (and ask the salesman about) the bait's density

and whether it will lie lightly on top of weed or fall through. Think about various colours and how they will relate to the colour of the bottom the bait is presented over. Will they blend in naturally or stand out. Think about the flavour. Do you want one which is used regularly on the water you fish because the carp have become accustomed to it, but also possibly scared by it through being caught too many times? Or is an entirely new and unknown flavour more likely to score once several pre-baiting sessions have accustomed the carp to a different food source?

These are the questions you should consider when purchasing pre-made boilies, and if you are not entirely happy then simply make you own. Bait suppliers not only provide all the component parts, they also give suggested recipes.

A comparatively new invention in the history of carp baits, and marketed only since the 1980s, ready-made boilies are available in a staggering variety of colours, flavours and sizes.

CHAPTER SIX

TECHNIQUES AND RIGS

FREELINING

If you spend any time at all observing carp and how they relate to a baited hook, you will soon understand why the simple method of freelining the bait without any foreign bits on the line (floats, shots, bombs, tubing, etc), other than the hook, is the most sensitive method of all. Unless the carp picks up the line with its large pectoral or pelvic fins, or brushes up against it and does a runner, it will trundle confidently off with the bait as though your hook did not exist.

To freeline any further out than a few yards, the bait needs to be reasonably heavy; the insides of a swan mussel, a cube of meat, a large lump of paste or bread flake, a 20 mm boilie and so on. In all cases, the hook by comparison weighs next to nothing. So unless the carp is aware of your presence, or is wary of the bait itself in which case it might quickly snatch and blow it out with equal speed (sometimes a quick strike when watching this happen will score), a confident bite usually occurs. If you cannot see the bait being taken, which is probably the case more often than not, keep your eyes glued to the line. Never be tempted to straighten the way in which it hangs between the rod tip and surface in a gentle bow, or how it lies loosely on the surface, because this in effect is your bite indicator.

When the line twitches (as the carp sucks in the bait), and then starts to straighten or simply tightens across the surface without any prior warning, there is no finer or more positive indication of a confident bite. Whenever carp are in the immediate area and might literally pick the bait up at any second, I rarely put the rod down. If, however, a long wait seems imminent the rod may be carefully laid on marginal plants with an ever-watchful eye kept on the line, or put in two rests with the tip pointed at the bait.

If, due to light patterns, dense undergrowth and so on, the line beyond the rod tip cannot be easily seen, use a light, simple, bobbin indicator on the line between reel and butt ring. A coil of silver foil (see 'Indicators' p. 57) is perfect because an exciting 'rustle' is often heard as the foil lifts upwards when the line tightens. At a pinch, squeeze a piece of bread on the line. When a carp takes the bait and moves towards the rod the line usually falls slack. These 'dropbacks' are in fact just as confident as 'forward' runs and should be struck immediately.

In lakes or pits with uneven bottoms where the line between bait and rod tip may come to rest amongst a patch of soft weed or between the stones on a gravel bar, dropback bites do not always register. For this reason, and because distance is anyway restricted as only the bait provides weight for casting, the method of freelining should be considered a technique for close-range fishing, say distances of up to no more than 25–30 yd.

I find freelining most effective for carp inhabiting smallish, weedy overgrown lakes and pits where casting with float or ledger tackle is particularly awkward. At spots that are too limited in marginal space for setting up rod rests and so on, freelining can be a very mobile technique. You can keep on the move seeking new swims, plopping the bait into all the promising-looking areas and resting the bait on the bottom for a minute or so before recasting to each new spot. In high summer, early in the morning or at dusk when carp are most likely to be continually on the move, sport can sometimes even prove instant. Watch the line from the moment the bait hits the surface for those aggressive and sudden takes on the drop, when from nothing the line tightens at speed.

Don't be afraid to be continually casting – there are times when impatience is just as important as patience. Try not to plop a bait directly above a patrolling group of carp. Place it well to the side so its entry will not scare them but its slow free fall to the bottom will not go unnoticed, perhaps tempting one of them to intercept it. Freelined baits may even be cast directly into weed beds such as lilies, because there is nothing to get caught on them. Its simplicity is its secret.

There is no one particular bait which works best when freelined, but in terms of preference I would rate heavy naturals like mussels, a bunch of cockles, a large cube of meat or large lobworms as the best for presenting on the bottom. Slow-sinking (flattened) pieces of paste (trout pellet paste) or breadflake encourage bites on the drop.

Opposite: Freeline tactics used in conjunction with an electric indicator, with the bait placed close in alongside the beds of marginal rushes, accounted for this lively, early morning carp.

FLOAT FISHING

The vast majority of experienced anglers would recognize float fishing as the most sensitive and effective method of presentation because the fish (whatever the species) feels the absolute minimum of resistance when it sucks in the bait and pulls the float under. Yet these same anglers share a mental blockage when contemplating catching carp on

Not all specimen carp are taken by ledgering high-protein boilies at long range. John took this superb leather carp on float-fished peanuts directly beneath the rod tip in just 3 ft of water. Even to get within casting distance of such fish, the prerequisites are stealth and observation.

float tackle. Why? I only wish I knew, because the plain truth is that carp are no different from any other species and fall readily to all float-fishing techniques.

It is true to say of course that big, old, crafty carp living in crystal-clear water are often scared by a vertical line stretched between the float and the bottom shots. But then, they are also scared by a ledgered line set horizontally anywhere from 1 in to 2 ft above the bottom, especially those wound up tight as a bow string, because in their world nothing beneath the surface is ever that rigid. All sub-surface plants bend to their bodies as they pass between the stems, which is why carp are quick to panic off, giving those sudden eruptions in shallow water that we call 'liners', when they bump into a tight line.

There are plus and minus points for each and every technique. However, let me seriously suggest that, armed with a selection of varying float rigs, you will be far better equipped to tackle carp wherever they live than you will be with the knowledge of just one modern-day ledgering rig such as the bolt rig (which is the case with so many of today's carp enthusiasts, who only ever associate catching the species with heavy lead rigs [see 'Ledgering', p. 112]).

Simple float rig

To start with, let's consider a simple float rig for offering a bait close into really shallow, possibly heavily reeded, margins where ledgering might easily spook patrolling carp. Even if the sound waves of a heavy lead going in doesn't scare them, the line stretched 'hauser' fashion from bait to rod tip most certainly will. They simply fade away when they sense the line or bump accidentally into it, and promptly vacate the area in blind panic. Neither occurrence is conducive to seeing a fat carp in the bottom of the net, and to overcome this consider the float rig in fig. 11 designed for *Laying on*. Simply attach 1 in of peacock quill (a tiny waggler will do nicely) to the line with a silicone rubber band at each end. After tying on the hook, set the float well overdepth so that at least 3 ft of line lies along the bottom. Then fix on a small shot (a no. 1) below the float, slightly deeper than the swim. The rod may then be placed in two rests or held.

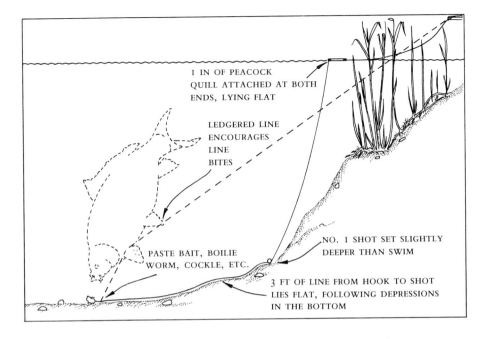

I IN OF PEACOCK QUILL ATTACHED AT BOTH ENDS, LYING FLAT

LEDGERED LINE ENCOURAGES LINE BITES

NO. I SHOT SET SLIGHTLY DEEPER THAN SWIM

PASTE BAIT, BOILIE WORM, COCKLE, ETC.

3 FT OF LINE FROM HOOK TO SHOT LIES FLAT, FOLLOWING DEPRESSIONS IN THE BOTTOM

The point of not having the float cocked is that water displacement caused by a carp's tail could move the line and dip the float momentarily (the float sometimes 'twitches' when fish are in the swim) and entice you into striking when there is no bite. When a carp does move off with the bait there is absolutely no messing. The float positively sinks from view as the line from bait to rod tip straightens.

FIGURE 11 *Laying on*

Lift rigs

For fishing deeper swims over gravel ledges, immediately over or between beds of lilies, potomogeton, dwarf pond lily or amphibious bistort, increase the peacock stem to 2 in long and fix the bottom end only to create a *mini lift rig* (fig. 12). Pinch a swan shot on lightly (so it comes off easily if the fish ploughs through weed) 3 in from the hook and set the float slightly overdepth so it cocks easily when you tighten up. I find that it is imperative to hold the rod in order to use the 'mini lift' effectively. Sometimes bites consist of a gentle, mere 'lifting' or slow 'sinking' of the quill, seemingly not the kind of bite associated with a double-figure carp. But, and this is what float fishing as

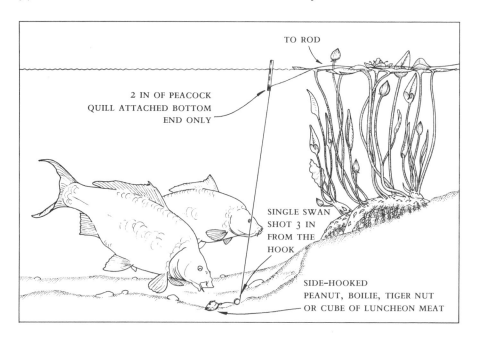

TO ROD

2 IN OF PEACOCK
QUILL ATTACHED BOTTOM
END ONLY

SINGLE SWAN
SHOT 3 IN
FROM THE
HOOK

SIDE-HOOKED
PEANUT, BOILIE, TIGER NUT
OR CUBE OF LUNCHEON MEAT

FIGURE 12 *Mini lift rig*

opposed to ledgering quickly teaches you, carp much of the time bite very delicately indeed because they are deliberate in their movements. It really depends on their mood at the time, because on occasions the float will just carry on going with such speed the fish does in fact hook itself. The 'mini lift' works wonderfully when presenting side-hooked particles or cubes of meat, etc. over loose-feed attractors like hempseed or tares.

Carp bubbling contentedly in the margins between beds of lilies are not too happy about a 2 oz lead landing amongst them. This is where float-fishing techniques, and in particular the lift method, are so effective. Very often a bait can be accurately placed and a carp hooked in less time than it has taken to write this.

Youngsters especially love the intrigue and visual excitement of float fishing for carp. They catch quality fish, too, as young · Jonathan Ross proved with this superb 15 lb common, beaten on just 6 lb test.

For presenting the bait accurately, yet at a reasonable distance out from the margins where carp are bubbling away in coloured water over loose feed or alongside lilies, increase the quill length to at least 6 in and pinch on two swan shots 4 in from the hook. With the *lift rig* (fig. 13) bites will now register in an unbelievably positive way, the buoyant quill rising quickly above the surface and keeling right over. Or the float tip will perhaps 'dither' for a second or two (as the carp blows the bait in and out) before vanishing completely. Either way, an instant strike is imperative so don't be tempted to put the rod down. Modern carp rods are very light, and besides, you would not think twice about holding a 13 ft trotting rod to fish a river for several hours, so why not hold the carp rod too. Actually holding the rod stops you getting lazy, always a danger in carp fishing when the action is slow, and keeps

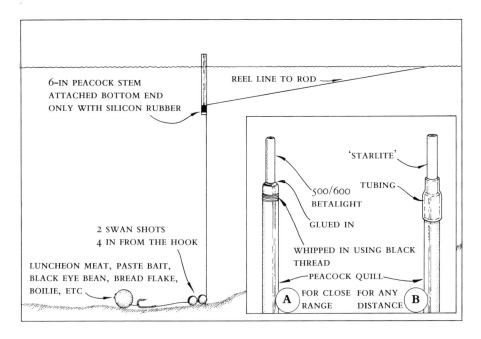

6-IN PEACOCK STEM
ATTACHED BOTTOM END
ONLY WITH SILICON RUBBER

REEL LINE TO ROD

'STARLITE'

500/600   TUBING
BETALIGHT

GLUED IN

2 SWAN SHOTS
4 IN FROM THE HOOK

WHIPPED IN USING BLACK
THREAD

LUNCHEON MEAT, PASTE BAIT,
BLACK EYE BEAN, BREAD FLAKE,
BOILIE, ETC

PEACOCK QUILL

A FOR CLOSE FOR ANY B
   RANGE   DISTANCE

FIGURES 13 AND 14
13 *Lift rig* and 14 *Lift
float fishing at night*

your mind alert. It makes you impatient for a bite, which is a good thing because opportune carp are the essence of float fishing.

Lift float fishing at night

Carp which inhabit very clear waters, or lakes and pits where marginal cover is sparse, are more inclined to feed close into the bank under the cloak of darkness. They then become nicely catchable with the lift method. Use a peacock quill fitted with a luminous element so that you can see the float easily.

For fishing close in just beyond the rod tip, and regular sessions at night, it pays to invest in a 500/600 micro-lambert (the most powerful) betalight luminous element, which is easily glued and whipped into the top of a peacock stem (fig. 14).

For the occasional night trip, and for fishing out well beyond the rod tip, use a 'standard' luminous 'starlite' chemical element which is very bright but lasts only for eight hours. It is easily slipped on to the tip of the peacock quill with a short length of clear tubing which comes supplied with the element.

Hair rigs

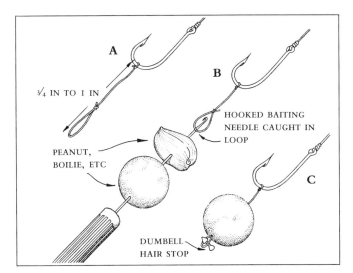

FIGURE 15 *Adding hair to hook (on lift rig)*

Returning to daytime fishing again, when bites are not forthcoming on the lift rig, but fish are obviously in the swim attracted by the loose feed, you can make the hook bait more appealing and easier to suck up without the carp feeling the initial weight and presence of the hook by threading the bait on to a 'hair'. Though developed for ledger rigs, the 'hair' works perfectly well when float fishing, whatever the technique. It is simply a short length of fine (¾ lb test) monofilament or black dacron (fly-tying thread is perfect and very cheap). Tie a tiny loop at one end and with a six-turn half blood knot tie the other end to the bend of the hook. In total the hair should be roughly between ¾ and 1 inch long, no more; although there is room for experiment here (see fig. 15A). Having sleeved the bait on to a 'hooked' baiting needle (fig. 15B) catch on to the loop and gently slide the bait on to the hair. To stop it from sliding off pop a tiny plastic hair stop into the loop (fig. 15C) and that's it.

Float ledger rig

To convert the *lift* into a *bolt rig* (or *shock rig*) with or without the bait on a 'hair', simply pinch on four or five

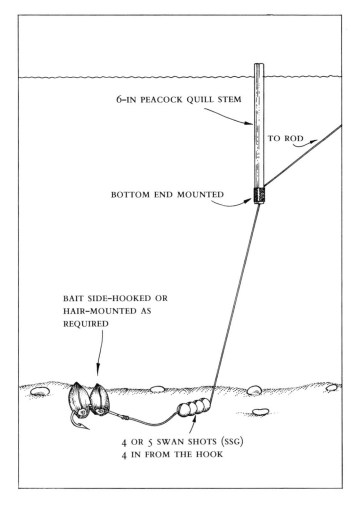

swan shot instead of the usual two (fig. 16). This invariably stops nuisance fish like bream and tench from pushing the bait about and giving false bites. Be prepared to hold the rod all the time because it is rather tricky fishing, especially with the bait close to lilies or beside jungle swims. When a carp grabs the bait and instantly panics off (hence the name shock or bolt rig), it feels the extra shots as the hook pricks home and it moves at incredible speed.

Converting the standard 'lift' method into a bolt rig is in fact far more practical for tackling weedy or lily-bed swims than ledgering and waiting for a buzzer to sound. Using a float (once you have accepted the fact that the rod must always be held) you can be walking slowly back-

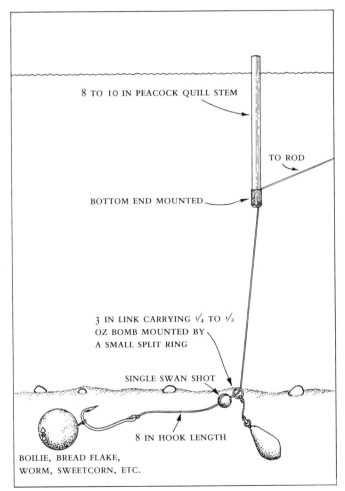

FIGURE 17 *Float ledger rig for distant swims*

8 TO 10 IN PEACOCK QUILL STEM

TO ROD

BOTTOM END MOUNTED

3 IN LINK CARRYING ¼ TO ½ OZ BOMB MOUNTED BY A SMALL SPLIT RING

SINGLE SWAN SHOT

8 IN HOOK LENGTH

BOILIE, BREAD FLAKE, WORM, SWEETCORN, ETC.

wards and bullying a big fish out of tough lily roots at least several seconds quicker than is needed for your brain to react to the noise of a bite alarm and tell your arm to strike, by which time of course the carp has wound 10 yd of line through the lily bed and is probably out through the other side.

To reach distant swims but still enjoy watching a float (not always a practicable technique in windy conditions) thread on a mini running ledger using a ¼ or ½ oz bomb and stop 8 in from the hook with a single swan shot (fig. 17). This simple float ledger rig also works well in deep water swims that are fairly close in to the bank at times when choppy conditions make light float fishing impossible.

Float fishing for crucians

To catch crucians regularly, a very carefully shotted light float rig is imperative, the best floats being a fine tipped antenna or a short, narrow-diameter length of peacock quill fished in 'mini lift' style. The object is to see those tiny bites for which crucians are renowned and which often barely register on the float tip (fig. 18).

For this reason the single shot (a no. 1, BB or AA depending on float size) should be not more than 2 in from the hook. Try moving it even closer, to 1 in away, because sometimes this alone can make all the difference between

FIGURES 18 AND 19
18 (right) *Mini lift rig for crucians* and 19 (left) *float fishing for crucians*

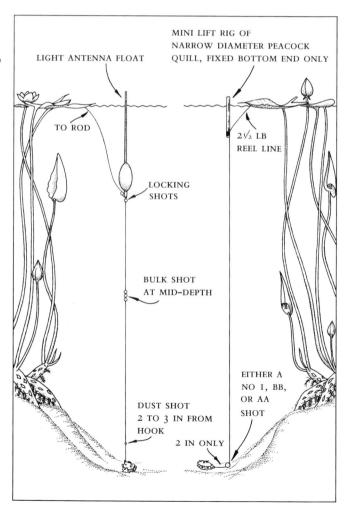

LIGHT ANTENNA FLOAT

MINI LIFT RIG OF
NARROW DIAMETER PEACOCK
QUILL, FIXED BOTTOM END ONLY

TO ROD

2 ½ LB
REEL LINE

LOCKING
SHOTS

BULK SHOT
AT MID-DEPTH

EITHER A
NO 1, BB,
OR AA
SHOT

DUST SHOT
2 TO 3 IN FROM
HOOK

2 IN ONLY

seeing bites and not. The secret, after casting in and tightening up so the float cocks, is to wind down even further so the tip is just the merest 'blimp' on the surface. And then strike the slightest movement whether it moves up or down.

When crucians are really feeding confidently (see 'Feeding'), denoted by clusters of small bubbles regularly rising to the surface, the float might even lift completely out of the water and lay flat, as the carp tilts its head up after sucking up the bait and dislodges the shot. Or the tip will sink positively as the crucian characteristically runs along the bottom. But far more bites will barely register on the float, so you need to hold the rod throughout and be eagle-eyed.

To stand a better chance of hitting bites from crafty crucians which just lie on the bottom blowing the bait in and out, rig up a light antenna float with a dust shot 2–3 in from the hook, the bulk shot set at mid depth (fig. 19). After carefully plumbing the swim, adjust the float so the bait is literally a fraction above the bottom. As with the lift rig, strike at the slightest movement on the float tip. Remember to keep loose feed or small balls of ground bait going in on the little-and-often principle, and they might be encouraged to feed all day. A ruse always worth trying when they are particularly dour is to gently wind the float in 6 in at a time, which makes the bait lift upwards enticingly and gently fall down to the bottom again. Baits which are inherently buoyant like breadflake or casters, or which are expected to move such as worms, work best when 'twitching' in this way to encourage bites.

FLOATER FISHING

Margin fishing

To catch carp slurping down floating baits like crusts or mixers which have either been scattered amongst the marginal growth or drifted there with the wind, there cannot be a more simple rig than using just the hook itself. If the fish are directly below the rod tip, lower the floater down so it rests on the surface without any slack line

The best rig for crucian carp: a single shot just 2 in from the hook, and a short length of peacock quill attached to the line with silicone tubing, fished lift style.

Crucians are always willing to feed, and can still be caught during the heat of a bright summer's day. Bites will appear as the tiniest registration on the float. To help combat this and reduce unwanted glare wear polaroid glasses and a sun vizor.

Even modest-sized carp provide long, exciting scraps when hooked close in. Overhanging tree canopies are the kind of spots beneath which carp feel totally confident in rising to suck in floaters.

lying on the water. Hold the rod loosely yet expectantly with the reel's bale arm closed (the clutch properly set), and in the other hand hold a loop of line pulled from between butt ring and reel (fig. 20). This you let slip through your fingers when a carp closes its mouth over the bait and submerges with it, before whacking the rod back to set the hook.

Many carp anglers would rate this particular form of marginal floater fishing as the most exciting technique of all and I would certainly not give them an argument. It is extremely satisfying, but demands tremendous stealth simply crawling into a position where a bait can be lowered amongst patrolling surface-feeding fish.

When surface activity is slow and the appearance of carp is not expected until the light starts to fade (either due to weather or clear water conditions) quietly set the rod on

LOOP OF LINE LOOSELY HELD

BALE ARM CLOSED

BAIT FLOATS ON THE SURFACE
WITHOUT ANY LINE LYING ON THE WATER   BAIT CAN BE CRUST, MIXER BISCUIT, ETC
TO SCARE THE CARP

FIGURE 20 *Margin
fishing (daytime)*

two rests, again with the bale arm closed, and instead of
holding the loop of line between butt ring and reel, hang
on a lightweight coil indicator. A cylinder of silver foil is
perfect (fig. 21).

When fishing this method over marginal lilies, wind the
bait so it comes to rest alongside the pads and lay the line
over them (fig. 22). Don't for a moment imagine the carp
cannot see even small floaters presented in this way. They
are looking up into bright light, and can even identify the
form of a floater resting completely on top of a lily pad.
On numerous occasions I have witnessed carp knocking
pads to dislodge a seemingly invisible (to them) unreachable

CLOSED BALE ARM

SILVER FOIL CYLINDER
ON LINE BETWEEN BUTT
RING AND REEL

LINE IS KEPT CLEAR OF WATER
TO PREVENT IT SCARING CARP

floater. And they are not satisfied until such food is in their stomachs.

FIGURE 21 *Margin fishing (dusk onwards)*

When using pieces of floating bread-crust over pads, or drifting them across the surface in open areas, if carp are suspicious of the floating bread use a crust/flake cocktail.

Start by sliding a piece of crust up over the eye of the hook and then squeeze on a giant piece of flake. Slide the crust down again and gently squeeze a part of the flake on to the crust, thus 'locking' them together. Hopefully they will hold together until a carp investigates and 'knocks' them apart, whereupon the flake will slowly start to sink. At this point the carp can stand it no longer and promptly

FIGURE 22 *Fishing*
over lilies

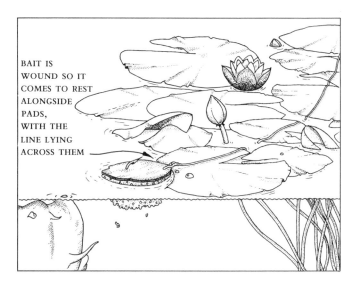

BAIT IS
WOUND SO IT
COMES TO REST
ALONGSIDE
PADS,
WITH THE
LINE LYING
ACROSS THEM

sucks in the flake. Watch the line carefully and hit any positive movement instantly.

Floating controllers

When carp will only accept floaters presented further out because the water along the margins is either too clear, too shallow or both, making them feel vulnerable, casting weight is required in the form of a self-cocking controller (see 'Tackle') like the 'ten-pin', which is available in two sizes, one for distances up to 30 yd, and a larger one for much greater distances. Loose-feed floaters like small biscuits, boilies and so on can all be catapulted into any given area alongside features, and the hook bait deposited accurately among them. Or better still, cast out the controller and hook bait well up wind; then catapult the loose feed around it, allowing the floating food to drift down wind whilst playing out line from an open (well-filled) spool.

Rig up a 'ten-pin' by threading the reel line (which should be liberally greased with mucilin so it floats well) through the swivel. Then thread on a small bead and tie on the hook. Anywhere from 2 to 6 ft above the hook, tie on a sliding stop knot against which the bead and finally the controller will come to rest (fig. 23A). Alternatively, after threading on the tenpin and bead, tie on a small swivel and

This young fisherman looks deservedly happy with a superbly conditioned common carp. It was taken on a small cube of bread crust presented with a 'ten-pin' loaded controller.

FIGURE 23 *Floating controllers*

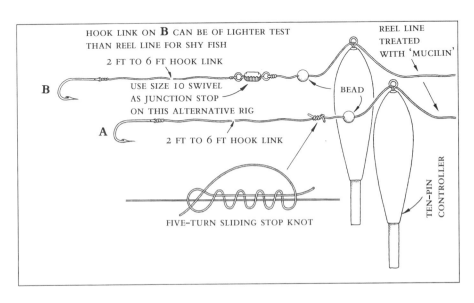

HOOK LINK ON **B** CAN BE OF LIGHTER TEST THAN REEL LINE FOR SHY FISH

2 FT TO 6 FT HOOK LINK

REEL LINE TREATED WITH 'MUCILIN'

B

USE SIZE 10 SWIVEL AS JUNCTION STOP ON THIS ALTERNATIVE RIG

BEAD

A

2 FT TO 6 FT HOOK LINK

FIVE-TURN SLIDING STOP KNOT

TEN-PIN CONTROLLER

to its other end add the hook link. This may be lighter than the reel line (if carp are really spooky), and anywhere from 2 to 6 ft long – even 10 ft long if you can cast it. Start with a 4 ft long hook link, however, for easy casting and finish the rig by adding the hook (fig. 23B). For large baits use hook sizes 6 to 8, while small floaters are more naturally presented on a strong, forged, size 10 or even size 12 provided conditions allow.

Tactics

Carp are invariably more wary of accepting surface baits once they have associated them with danger than they are of bottom-fished baits. But by fishing as light as you dare, using much finer line than normal, for instance 6 lb test instead of 10 lb test if conditions permit, and by fishing during periods of low light at dusk, dawn or even well on into darkness, most problems can be solved. Carp refuse the bait because they can see the line and hook, or because the bait behaves unlike all the free offerings around it due to the weight of the hook and drag from the line. Carp prove this time and time again by mopping up all the free floaters, but not the one on the hook. It is frustration personified. The problem is not so much getting them to accept floating food but to accept the hook bait. Even familiar unattached baits like pieces of bread crust are taken down, maybe not so quickly on waters regularly fished, but disappear they eventually will. Particle baits create far less suspicion, and sooner or later one will be sucked in, provided carp respond.

In contrast to bottom baits, at least it's possible to actually observe the reaction of carp and consequently do something about the way in which the bait is refused. Anything and everything is worth trying. Go for a much longer hook link to create less drag; or smaller hook; two floaters instead of one, which provides greater buoyancy; grease or even degrease the hook link, and so on.

If all else fails, put your faith in the hair rig (fig. 24) and offer the bait off the hook. Rig the floater up sleeved on to a fine mono or dacron 1 in hair, and support the hook so it floats horizontally on the surface by threading a length of 3 mm duplon (rod-handle material) on to the shank. There

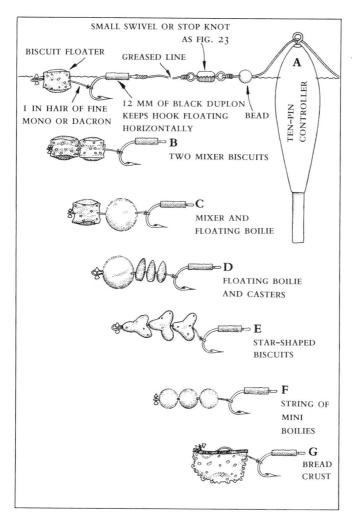

FIGURE 24 *Hair-rig floaters*

are all sorts of variations worth trying along these lines. Go down in hook size: try two or even three floaters on the hair instead of one; or a cocktail, one biscuit and one boilie together on the same hair, a boilie and casters, and so on.

Offering a floating bait is perhaps the most selective of all big carp methods, because you can actually watch the fish of your dreams close its great lips over the bait. You can even pull the bait away from lesser fish should the commotion of hooking one scare off a monster which is one amongst a group of modest-sized carp.

Because the line actually passes through the top of the controller, when a carp moves away with the bait the line

There is nothing too deliberate or choosy about the way in which these two mirror carp are munching through a batch of dog-biscuit floaters. When they eventually wise up to floaters presented straight on the hook, offer the bait on a fine hair rig.

will visibly tighten and 'lift' across the surface. Hold the rod all the time with the bale arm closed ready for action. Straighten any bow in the line formed by wind drift, leaving just a little slack so as not to scare interested fish through resistance. Keep your eyes fixed on the float's red top and identify your hook bait amongst the loose ones, striking on sight if you suddenly see it go without the line actually moving or whistling through the float.

Not all carp belt off. Some merely sink slowly beneath the surface and munch merrily away. Remember the controller float is not designed to go under, simply to take the bait out anywhere from 10 to 50 yd. At distances beyond this, casting and wind drift problems hamper float control and striking.

Fishing at distance

The answer to distance problems is the *anchored floater* presented on a sliding, buoyant paternoster rig (fig. 25). Retain the 4 ft hook link and swap the float for a long paternoster link consisting of a 1½ oz bomb at the bottom and a swivel at the top, with a buoyant sub-float body which slides freely in between. A buoyant bead up against

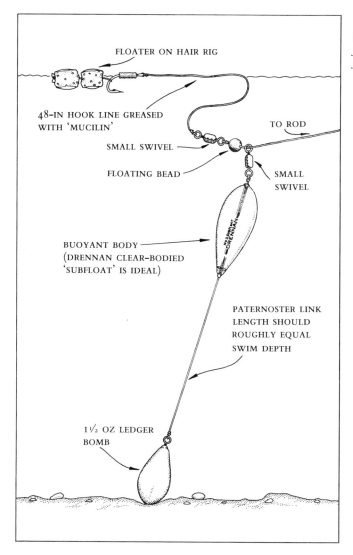

FLOATER ON HAIR RIG

48-IN HOOK LINE GREASED
WITH 'MUCILIN'

TO ROD

SMALL SWIVEL

FLOATING BEAD

SMALL
SWIVEL

BUOYANT BODY
(DRENNAN CLEAR-BODIED
'SUBFLOAT' IS IDEAL)

PATERNOSTER LINK
LENGTH SHOULD
ROUGHLY EQUAL
SWIM DEPTH

1½ OZ LEDGER
BOMB

FIGURE 25 *Anchored
floater for distance
fishing*

the small junction swivel helps flotation. This link should measure approximately the depth of the swim. When the rig lands and the bomb touches bottom, the buoyant float body rises up to the swivel and supports the reel line just a couple of feet below the surface with the bait floating nicely above.

Tighten up gently with the rod set horizontal in two rests, ensuring the line is sunk, and clip on an indicator, such as bobbin or monkey climber. Keep the bale arm closed. When a carp sucks in the floater, the reel line runs freely through the paternoster swivel, up goes the indicator and you are in business with a hefty strike to pick up any loose line.

For this kind of long-range floater fishing, keep your eyes peeled on the area of the hook bait with binoculars so you can anticipate a probable run if you sight carp in the vicinity, and use wind direction plus your catapult to scatter loose floaters around the anchored hook bait.

LEDGERING

A basic multi-purpose rig

FIGURE 26 *A basic multi-purpose rig (the running link ledger)*

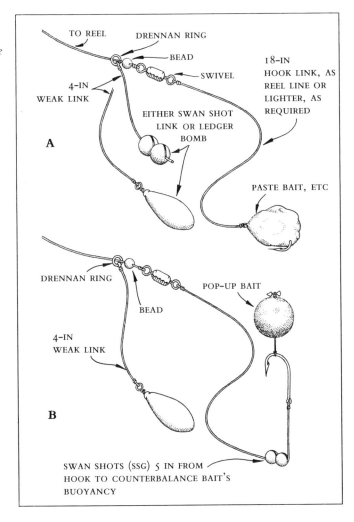

For ledgering pieces of soft paste, cubes of meat, perhaps a couple of cockles, in diminutive waters where belt-off runs are neither expected nor desired, use a simple running link ledger as in fig. 26A.

Where a carp could go ploughing through weeds or snags, the ledger link, to which is attached a small bomb or swan shots, should be of a considerably lighter test than the reel line. Thus it creates a weak link which will break off when caught up in weeds, leaving the carp still connected to the main line.

FIGURE 27 *A heavier multi-purpose rig*

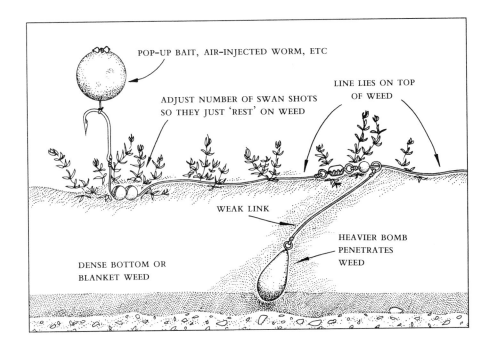

For presenting pop-up baits, such as an air-injected lobworm or any of the floating baits (usually fished on the surface), fix on one or two swan shots 5 in from the hook to counterbalance the bait's buoyancy as in fig. 26B.

When fishing over dense bottom or blanket weed simply extend the ledger link to compensate, and use a heavier bomb for penetration down to the bottom (fig. 27). Experiment in the margins where you can see the rig working until you are happy.

Scorching runs are sometimes experienced with this set-up should the rig become hung up in weed. Generally, however, the indicator (monkey climber or coil) rises

positively upwards, usually with enough time for an unhurried strike. Coupled to a buzzer the warning is quite adequate when sitting beside the rod. As I play fish from a pre-adjusted clutch, the anti-reverse is always on, enabling me at any point to grab the rod one-handed if necessary without the handle whizzing round.

Opposite: *Admiring the carp before carefully returning it is all part of the enjoyment.*

The bolt rig

Now we arrive at what in recent years has become the panacea to catching carp: the *bolt* or *shock rig* ledger. Sadly, people use no other technique because it is so effective. I have left the bolt rig until last because I wish you, the reader, to treat its use as such: a 'deadly' method for catching 'difficult carp' – carp which are so wary they won't provide enough indications on other methods of presentation for you to strike and hook them. These other methods of varying skill and technique, most of which have already been covered, open up the entire exciting carp fishing world and enable you to value and catch carp of all shapes and sizes from a diverse variety of fisheries. The bolt rig also allows you this enjoyment, and at the end of the day you choose that which provides the most pleasure.

It's a fact that carp do not fall for the same tackle rig time after time. Bites which started out as slammers on simple ledger tackle soon become 'twitches', so imperceptible they are impossible to strike. And this is when the 'bolt rig' comes into its own. Using a heavy lead ($1\frac{1}{2}$ to 2 oz) which is felt by the carp just as it sucks the bait from the bottom back to its throat teeth for chewing, shocks that carp into closing its lips and doing a runner. In short it 'bolts off'. In the process it forgets about the bait and the hook is pulled home. The secret is in having exactly the right distance from lead to bait, which obviously varies with different-sized carp.

A distance somewhere between 6 to 10 in from hook to lead is favoured. The bait (boilies and hard particles such as beans or peanuts, etc., work best with this method) can simply be side-hooked (fig. 28A) or slid on to a 'hair' (fig. 28B), providing the carp with extra confidence when it sucks it in. In each case the hook link can be of monofilament (reel line), black or multi-coloured dacron

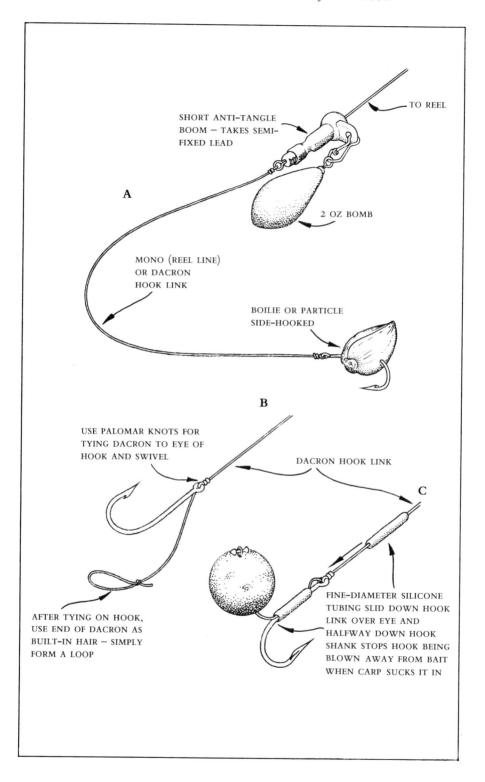

TO REEL

SHORT ANTI-TANGLE
BOOM – TAKES SEMI-
FIXED LEAD

2 OZ BOMB

A

MONO (REEL LINE)
OR DACRON
HOOK LINK

BOILIE OR PARTICLE
SIDE-HOOKED

B

USE PALOMAR KNOTS FOR
TYING DACRON TO EYE OF
HOOK AND SWIVEL

DACRON HOOK LINK

C

AFTER TYING ON HOOK,
USE END OF DACRON AS
BUILT-IN HAIR – SIMPLY
FORM A LOOP

FINE-DIAMETER SILICONE
TUBING SLID DOWN HOOK
LINK OVER EYE AND
HALFWAY DOWN HOOK
SHANK STOPS HOOK BEING
BLOWN AWAY FROM BAIT
WHEN CARP SUCKS IT IN

or braid, or of floss which separates into numerous gossamer strands and becomes virtually invisible on the bottom (see 'Hook lengths', p. 52).

With dacron hook lengths, after tying the hook on don't clip the end off short. Simply tie in a small loop and use it as a 'built in' hair.

To stop the hook being blown away from the bait when a carp sucks it in, sleeve a short length of fine-diameter clear or black silicone tubing down the hook link over the eye and onto the shank, thus shortening the hair length (fig. 28C).

Note from fig. 28A that the (semi-fixed) 2 oz lead is attached to the clip of a short boom which threads on to the reel line above the hook link swivel and stops the lead from tangling. There are numerous types of anti-tangle ledger rig bits now available, almost as much choice, in fact, as the match fisherman has in floats. Much of it is superfluous, and only helps to deter carp from approaching the bait. So my advice is to keep your terminal rig as simple as possible. With this in mind consider my 'simple bolt fig' in fig. 29. The short hook link and reel line are

FIGURE 28 (Opposite) *The bolt or shock rig*

FIGURE 29 *A simple bolt rig*

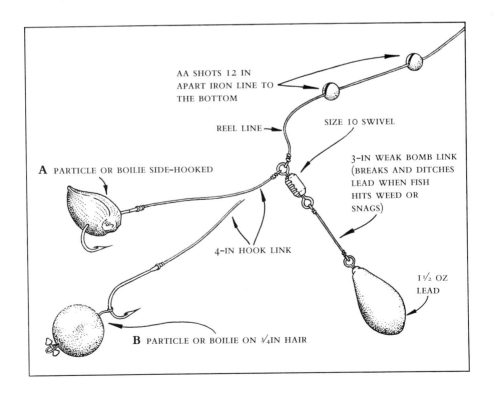

AA SHOTS 12 IN APART IRON LINE TO THE BOTTOM

REEL LINE

SIZE 10 SWIVEL

3-IN WEAK BOMB LINK (BREAKS AND DITCHES LEAD WHEN FISH HITS WEED OR SNAGS)

A PARTICLE OR BOILIE SIDE-HOOKED

4-IN HOOK LINK

1½ OZ LEAD

B PARTICLE OR BOILIE ON ¾IN HAIR

What every carp angler loves to see, fish rising freely to surface baits in a quiet corner of a beautiful lake.

both connected to the same end of a tiny size 10 swivel, so that should it break in half you are still playing the carp, while the 'weak' bomb link is tied to the other end of the swivel. Lengths of both hook and bomb links can be varied to suit bottom or weed of varying types, but overall a hook link of 4 in and a bomb link of 3 in are ideal.

The beauty of this rig is its 'simplicity', and the fact that should a carp go belting off through heavy weed the weak link soon ditches the lead. It is also excellent for presenting pop-up baits on the hair rig above dense bottom weed (see fig. 30). If the bottom weed is deeper than the 3 in lead link, simply alter it accordingly. Note the three AA shots pinched at 12 in intervals up the line from the swivels, which iron the reel line to the weed or hide it in soft silt so as not to scare carp as they approach the bait. To hide the reel line, dip the rod tip beneath the surface after casting, and with the left hand (assuming you are holding the rod in your right hand) gently pull the line until it is straight. Then allow a little slack from the reel and lift the rod horizontally on to the rests.

Opposite: The bolt rig/boilie combination presented 50 yd out on a shallow bar accounted for this fine Norfolk specimen.

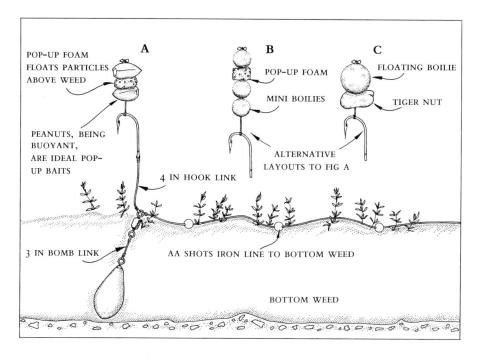

POP-UP FOAM
FLOATS PARTICLES
ABOVE WEED

A   **B**   **C**

POP-UP FOAM   FLOATING BOILIE

MINI BOILIES   TIGER NUT

PEANUTS, BEING
BUOYANT,
ARE IDEAL POP-
UP BAITS

ALTERNATIVE
LAYOUTS TO FIG A

4 IN HOOK LINK

3 IN BOMB LINK

AA SHOTS IRON LINE TO BOTTOM WEED

BOTTOM WEED

FIGURE 30 *Pop-up bolt rig*

Contrary to popular belief, the line from bolt rig to rod does not necessarily need to be 'hauser' tight in order for the hook point to be driven home. The lead in conjunction with the speed at which a carp panics off are responsible for this. So wherever possible leave a slight bow in the line from rod tip to surface. This means the line close to the bolt rig will be lying along the bottom contours and not inhibiting carp in crystal-clear water from approaching the bait.

There is perhaps a better hooking rate once the carp has picked up the bait presented on a 'tight line' from lead to rod. But if a proportion of runs do not happen because the carp sensed the 'bowstring line' and departed, it does not help you catch more fish.

Whenever there is a strong undertow in large waters, as in windy conditions, it is of course impossible to fish a gentle bow. Then it has to be a tight line 'clipped up' or nothing. At the reel end, after putting the line beneath the 'monkey', open the bale arm and neatly catch the line beneath a run clip fixed around the handle directly opposite the spool (see fig. 31). When a carp grabs the bait and promptly does a runner, line spews from the open spool while the monkey body drops a couple of inches, held

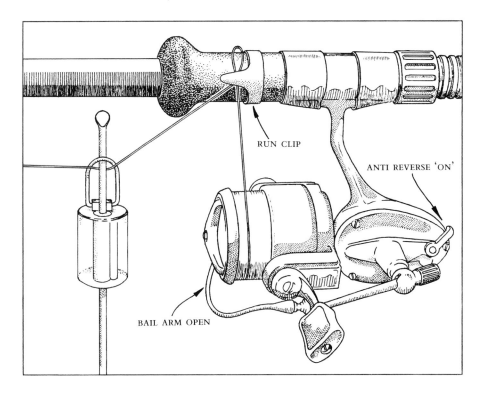

RUN CLIP

ANTI REVERSE 'ON'

BAIL ARM OPEN

there through the sheer speed of line evaporating from the open spool, while the buzzer screams its head off.

Figure 31 Clipping up the line

If using a reel with a bait runner facility, the bale arm will of course already be closed while the spool itself revolves. For both situations, a hefty strike is not required; indeed it could even prove disastrous. Simply close the bale arm by winding forward (which also puts the bait runner reel back into gear with a pre-set clutch) and gently bend the rod back into the fish when all is nicely tight. It is a very stereotyped and easy method to master.

In confined overgrown fisheries where the erection of rod rest set-ups, buzzers and monkey climbers could ruin the chances of carp even patrolling close by, let alone picking up a bolt-rigged bait-up, I fish in a very basic, effective, if rather risky way. As I never leave the rod or rods (I occasionally use two rods, though for much of my carp fishing, because it is based on opportunity rather than patience, I use just one) after placing the bait accurately and ensuring the line is nicely sunk along the bottom (hence my preference for two or three AA shots spread along the line above the lead), I simply lay the rod down on the

Whether you prefer fishing with the bait anchored to the bottom with a 3 oz lead, or feeling for bites in the dark with the line hooked around your index finger, there is no more exciting sight than observing carp confidently mopping up floaters from the surface.

carpet of marginal plants. I use no rod rests or alarms, but the anti-reverse is on and the clutch is set a shade lighter than I intend playing a fish with.

One minute there is nothing. The very next there is a furrow on the surface (if fishing shallow water) as a carp panics off, easily setting the hook and jerking the rod across the marginal plants in the process. I said it was a risky technique and indeed it is. But honestly, after taking goodness knows how many double-figure carp by this method from numerous fisheries, certainly well over 100, I have yet to be broken or to lose the rod. But it's not for the faint-hearted.

Good carping

INDEX